EXPONENTIAL POWER

For the Creative Design Entrepreneur & Professional

Handbook

NEW GUIDE AND THEORY TO ACHIEVEMENT BEYOND YOUR WILDEST DREAMS

Bjorn Christian Martinoff

Copyright © Bjorn C. Martinoff 2015

Copyright © 2015 by Bjorn C. Martinoff. All rights reserved.

Published by F1C International, Manila, Philippines.

No part of this publication may be reproduced, stored in a retrieval system, or transmitted in any form or by any means, electronic, mechanical, photocopying, recording, scanning, or otherwise, except as permitted under Section 107 or 108 of the 1976 United States Copyright Act, without either the prior written permission of the Publisher, or authorization through payment of the appropriate per-copy fee to the Publisher.

Requests to the Publisher for permission should be addressed to the Permissions Department, F1C International, 9719 Pililia Street #201, Makati City, Philippines, 1208, info@fortune100coach.com.

Telephone number: +632-478-3844

Limit of Liability/Disclaimer of Warranty: While the publisher and author have used their best efforts in preparing this book, they make no representations or warranties with respect to the accuracy or completeness of the contents of this book and specifically disclaim any implied warranties of merchantability or fitness for a particular purpose. No warranty may be created or extended by sales representatives or written sales materials. The advice and strategies contained herein may not be suitable for your situation. You should consult with a professional where appropriate. Neither the publisher nor author shall be liable for any loss of profit or any other damages, commercial or otherwise, including but not limited to special, incidental, consequential, or other damages.

Printed in the Philippines.

ISBN 978-0-692-42898-6

> *"He who controls others may be powerful, but he who has mastered himself is mightier still."*
>
> — LAO-TZU

For my wife Victoria, and my children Minday, Maxwell, Malcolm, and Sarah.

You are my sunshine.

You are my life.

CONTENTS

9 ACKNOWLEDGMENTS

10 PREFACE

14 INTRODUCTION

16   1. THE POWER OF ACTION
How to tell which actions are most fulfilling

21   2. THE POWER OF ALIGNMENT
How to triple your results without any extra effort

28   3. THE POWER OF AUTHENTICITY
How to cut through the smoke screen and get to the bottom line

32   4. THE POWER OF BELIEF
How what you believe can bring you to a screeching halt

37   5. THE POWER OF CHOICE
How to have a choice even when there isn't any

42   6. THE POWER OF COMMITMENT
The driving power behind your goals

DEVELOP EXPONENTIAL POWER

46   7. THE POWER OF CONTRIBUTION
Be energized by making a difference

51   8. THE POWER OF COURAGE
Expand then blow apart your limits

56   9. THE POWER OF DETACHMENT
Being open to something most often brings it

62   10. THE POWER OF EMPATHY
How to have instant access to someone's world

68   11. THE POWER OF FAITH
How to have certainty in uncertain times

72   12. THE POWER OF FLEXIBILITY
Getting what you want even when there are obstacles

77   13. THE POWER OF FOCUS
Your road sign to your destiny

82   14. THE POWER OF FUN
How to have more energy when you need it most

86   15. THE POWER OF GRATITUDE
What if being thankful is paying it forward?

CONTENTS

▬ DEVELOP EXPONENTIAL POTENTIAL

90 16. THE POWER OF GROWTH
How to accelerate your growth and supercharge your success

94 17. THE POWER OF HUMILITY
How being powerful and humble makes you unforgettable

98 18. THE POWER OF INSPIRATION
Self-motivate when it's needed most

102 19. THE POWER OF INTEGRITY
Without it nothing works

106 20. THE POWER OF INTERPRETATION
How to turn lead into gold

110 21. THE POWER OF LUCK
How to have more and on demand

114 22. THE POWER OF PEACE
The stability that brings about momentum

118 23. THE POWER OF PRESENCE
How to nurture it as a gift to others

122 24. THE POWER OF PURPOSE
Driven by WHY

128 25. THE POWER OF REALITY
Knowing where you are will tell you the directions

132 26. THE POWER OF RESPONSIBILITY
Victim or victor? The choice is yours

136 27. THE POWER OF TRUST
Opening doors the gentle way

140 28. THE POWER OF VISION
How being clear about what you want attracts it

143 AFTERWORD

144 ABOUT THE AUTHOR

145 SOME BOOK RECOMMENDATIONS

ACKNOWLEDGMENTS

Michael Beckwith says it takes a village to raise a child and I say it takes a village to inspire an author, or at least that's what it seemed to take for me. And so I'd like to thank and acknowledge all of those that have been an inspiration to me.

My special thanks and gratitude go to my wife Victoria and our wonderful children. You are the light of my life. I thank you for your trust and patience, without it this workbook would not have been possible.

I also like to thank Rev. Dr. Michael Beckwith, Neale Donald Walsch, Marianne Williamson, Anthony Robbins, Werner Erhard, L. Ron Hubbard, the Forum Leaders of Landmark Education and my many other teachers for their wonderful, wonderful inspiration.

I want to thank my many coaches for their great support over the years. They are my dear friends Nika Solomon, Cristelle Morrison, Roderick Sun, Aljor Perreras, Christine Garcia, and Darrel Gurney. You supported me when I was not yet on the map. I thank you.

Thank you also to my wonderful and hardworking Editor Eileen Tupaz. Without you this workbook may have taken a couple more years to complete.

Most of all I'd like to thank God, my ever loving and inspiring higher power and friend, for all the loving support when I most needed it and for sending your great Angels in the middle of the darkest time of my life.

PREFACE

BJORN MARTINOFF

At the everyday level of understanding, power refers to our ability to influence our environment and the behavior of other people. Basically it's about getting things done. Hundreds of books have been written on the subject—books whose success in the market testifies to a deeply felt need we all have to gain or develop this ability in ourselves. While power is often confused with force and manipulation, it is only true power, inner power, the power to control ourselves along with the appropriate beingness that truly enlivens and inspires others. True power therefore is not given or taken or manipulated. True power is lived, exuded from within, demonstrated and shared. For power to be expressed outwardly there are the three realms of actions; systems; and lastly, the paradigms, beingnesses, values and beliefs involved.

This workbook focuses mostly on the beingnesses required to achieve exponential power.

While other books offer invaluable insights on getting things done your way, they tend to emphasize scenarios where the application of power is often simply a limited and disguised form of manipulation.

True power is not the forceful imposition of one's will onto another, nor is it manipulation. At the heart of manipulation lies the fear that one is not be powerful enough and one therefore needs to deploy some sort of farce, force or make-believe scenario that fools others into compliance. While these tactics may get results, they are much less satisfying in the end because in our hearts lies the knowledge that our victory was won through trickery. While we can fool others with these tactics, we can never fool ourselves.

For instance, many books on power focus on the general techniques that usually enhance it, such as promoting oneself, building networks and cultivating an image. And in many cases across the board, power tends to be used synonymously with force—a tool that somehow necessarily involves persuasion, manipulation and even deception.

Why the effectiveness of such principles can be limited is because:

(1) they foster the view that power is dependent on possessing a certain title, position or set of circumstances;
(2) they presume that people can remember and apply at the right moment all the hundreds and thousands of tips and

PREFACE

techniques that grant or maximize power in various situations; and

(3) by confusing power with force, they leave an impression that power is somehow inherently evil—an immoral capacity that we have to exercise simply because so much in our lives depends on it.

This workbook is based on entirely different premises. It proceeds from my beliefs that:

(1) access to power is an ability all human beings have;

(2) this ability can be developed to an extraordinary degrees by cultivating habitual ways of being rather than by memorizing routine ways of doing; and

(3) it is an ability that doesn't carry the negative connotations of force because it is distinct from force. Force "pushes" against resistance in order to make things happen, while power eludes resistance by using the "pull" of attraction and inspiration.

In other words, we all already possess a certain amount of power and we can develop it to any degree that we desire. Furthermore, it's an ability that doesn't necessarily involve any of the negative practices that are said to go with it: practices such as persuasion, manipulation and deception.

What this workbook therefore describes are the fundamental bases of power—ways of being in the world that generate power as a by-product rather than as a function of personality, circumstance or strategy. Ways of being transcend personality, are indifferent to circumstance, and ultimately underlie all strategy. They can therefore be applied by anyone at any time, place and situation without the usual constraint of having to act or behave in certain ways.

See, having to act or behave in certain ways falls under the domain of following "laws." Because people usually relate to power as the result of acting or behaving in particular ways, books about power often talk about the "laws" of power. But laws exist only when, and because, people don't live by a common set of values. If people lived by common values, no laws would be needed. The same notion applies to the so-called laws of power.

Why this workbook calls itself a guide to "exponential power" is because when the ways of being that generate power are practiced together, their cumulative effect is exponential. The ways of being described in this workbook are already enormously effective when applied individually—but what they provide when they're practiced in combination, rapid succession, or en masse is an unprecedented shift in your level of personal power that can hardly be grasped by merely reading about it. One will actually have to practice it to have a full grasp and understanding of the power that is about to be revealed to you.

The following graphics will illustrate the shifts generated by frequent and continuous shifts in beingness/values.

Graphic 1.1
Normal Growth:

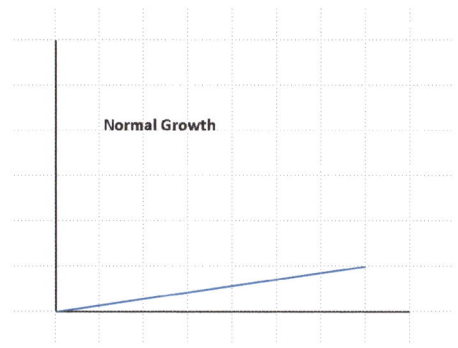

Graphic 2.1
Growth through upgraded skills:

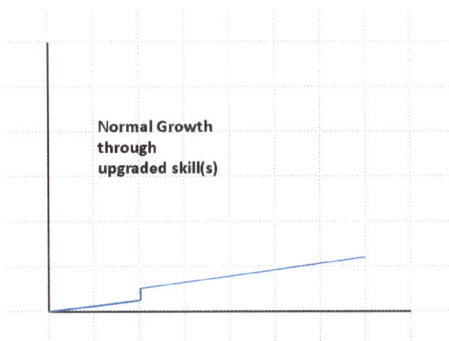

Graphic 3.1
Growth after Life Changing Impact:

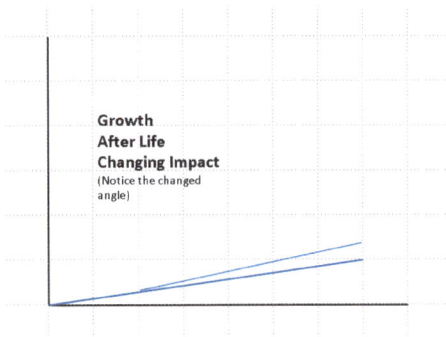

Here, the angle or trajectory of growth has taken on a new direction, which over time will make a major difference. While in the beginning the impact appears small, over time it becomes greater and greater compared with the original "normal" growth curve in Graphic 1.1.

Graphic 4.1
Exponential Power and Growth As a Result of repeated Life Changes in Being:

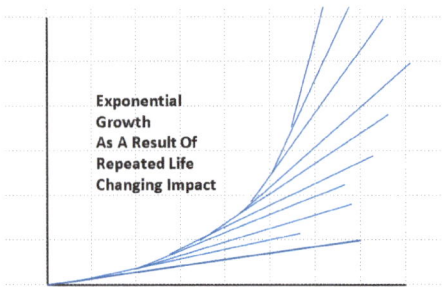

What is shown here is the impact on growth caused by frequently repeated life changing experiences, as well as shifts in beingness brought about by newly adopted values.

Graphic 5.1
Exponential Growth means Radical Results:

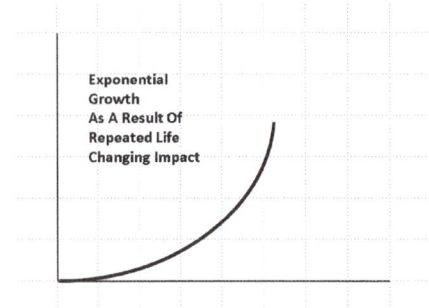

In Graphic 5.1 we have cleaned up the curve. It is now clearly visible how exponential growth can be made accessible to individuals. However this is also possible for teams and entire organizations.

Is exponential growth unusual? Not in nature. In nature everything grows exponentially. Plants grow exponentially. Exponential growth is not unusual at all. What is unusual, really, is when we think we can only grow at 4, 5, 6 or 10 percent per year.

Now, while the workbook proceeds by using simple and straightforward language, the content is actually a highly advanced conversation and may or may not be easily put into action in your life. Each chapter presents the opportunity to change your life in a significant way that can empower you exponentially. When combined, these teachings will help you grow exponentially as you translate each chapter from knowledge into action. We say knowledge is worthless, but I would say that "knowledge that isn't being used is worthless." Knowledge that is being put into action is highly valuable. So take caution: the knowledge you will gain from this workbook will make no difference. What will make a HUGE difference is APPLYING the knowledge that you will gain from this workbook. The difference that the application of this knowledge will make will be exponential.

All of this is accessible to people of various backgrounds and motivations—whether they be executives who have likely already read other books on power, or creative professionals such as yourself who may not have previously read anything on the subject matter.

Whatever your background or your motivation may be in reading or examining this workbook, it is designed to provide you with access to more power and the ability to access that power on an ongoing basis.

May you use it to become the master of your own destiny—and may you use the personal power you subsequently generate—wisely and for the good of all mankind.

INTRODUCTION

HOW TO USE THIS HANDBOOK

There is no right or wrong way to read this workbook. The way it is structured allows you, the creative professional, to choose between reading it straight from front to back, or, reading selected chapters as the need or inspiration arises.

Each chapter is devoted to a way of being that is sufficient in generating power in and by itself. Yet when the various principles are applied together (in twos, or threes, or even more), they exponentially increase the power that they make available to you.

Rather than relating to these ways of being, however, as yet another set of techniques to memorize, I encourage you, the reader, to cultivate them as habits instead. The virtue of a habit over a technique is that as an automatic reaction versus a deliberate response, it takes far less time and effort to apply a habit in a specific situation. For example, when you get out of bed, you proceed to brush your teeth through sheer force of habit—it is an action that no longer needs the time and effort of deliberate thought or intention.

The work that you have to do while reading this workbook therefore lies in getting habituated to the ways of being it recommends. One of the most effective ways of accomplishing this habituation is by reading or reviewing a chapter for a day (or a week) and then repeatedly performing its suggested exercise throughout the day (or the week).

At some point, the way of being will become a reflexive response, and generating power will become increasingly easier. It will certainly not be easy at the start (in the same way that brushing your teeth first thing in the morning may not have been easy at the start), but I promise you that the effort is worth it (as the current healthy state of your gums has proven).

Just a final word on applying the ways of being suggested in this workbook: take the principles that work for you and only the principles that work for you. But in order for you to determine which principles work for you or not, you have to test them thoroughly at least once. So try to proceed as a scientist would—with a spirit of genuine curiosity as to what will ultimately prove effective. You will not only discover things that may surprise you, but you will expand your capacity to generate power and results as well. And it's this, and only this, that is the intention of this workbook.

I promise you this workbook will serve you well.

"In life, understanding is the booby prize."

— WERNER ERHARD

1. THE POWER OF ACTION

WHAT WILL GIVE YOU WHAT YOU WANT

In life, there's only one way to generate any kind of result, and that's by taking action. The result you get depends on the kind of action you take. In general, there are three kinds of action: actions that create, actions that maintain and actions that destroy.

Actions that destroy are pretty straightforward. Where I find people getting confused is when it comes to actions that create and actions that maintain.

Very often, people spend their time and energy taking action to maintain something. They'll water the plants daily to maintain their garden, go to the gym weekly to maintain their health and visit their mothers monthly to maintain their relationship. What people don't realize, however, is that taking action to merely maintain something usually isn't very inspiring. In fact, it often ends up being work.

ARTWORK BY RENE TRINIDAD ALDONZA

That's why I assert that it's vitally important to keep our actions in the realm of creation. No matter how small an action might be, it's important to have it create something versus just keep something alive.

If you look back in your life, you'll understand what I'm talking about. Have you noticed, for instance, that you're always most excited and most enthusiastic at the beginning of a new creative project? It's like you're brimming with time, energy and ideas, and the results usually come fast. That's the power of creation as opposed to the power of preservation. But how, you ask, can you stay in the realm of creation without having to come up with new projects all the time? In fact, isn't it kind of fickle and irresponsible to keep coming up with new things?

Here's my answer: creating something new doesn't necessarily mean creating a new project. In fact, you can always create something new even with old or existing projects. It's the freshness and novelty that you inject into these projects by

Massive consistent action with pure persistence and a sense of flexibility in pursuing your goals will ultimately give you what you want."
— *ANTHONY ROBBINS*

creating something new that keeps you in the realm of excitement and inspiration.

For example, let's say that one project you've created in your life is to cook your own meals so that you can control your nutritional intake better. Just like any new project, this will excite you a lot in the beginning. But after days and weeks of taking the time and attention that's needed to prepare healthy food, this project will start becoming a chore—a clear sign that the actions have devolved to the level of maintenance. In the beginning it was new and exciting. It involved creating a new future, which is the work of a leader. Once that future was established, it became the work of a manager, which is to maintain things. Once you've tasted the excitement of being a leader, it may not be as exciting to become a manager. There is juice, power and energy in maintaining the excitement. Actions that can bring the project back into the realm of creation include things like:

(1) preparing a week's worth of meals without repeating a single dish;
(2) preparing meals just as good or healthy but at half the budget; and
(3) convincing someone else to eat healthily just by having them taste how good your dishes are!

The point is, in each of the actions I just gave as an example, something new was added to the project that wasn't there before—a new dimension or a new context that can provide a fresh source of motivation and inspiration. This is what I mean when I say that you can always keep your actions in the realm of creation without having to create new projects all the time.

The good news is, given that you're already in the creative field, you have more experience and skill in this area than the average person does. It's simply a matter of applying your creativity to areas of your life outside of your work!

In my own life, one example of an action I take in the realm of maintenance is to stay in touch with my clients even when my work or project with them is complete or even when I know that they're not in the space for an engagement. An action that would be in the realm of creation would be to continue to support them, whether paid or not, until such time when we can begin a new project.

Maintaining the contact gets me present to new challenges that my clients may be dealing with, which, in turn, gives me ideas on new ways that I can be of service. The same clients may or may not engage me for these services, but other potential clients might and do. This is an example of being able to continuously generate something new from something that is based on something that already exists.

And just by doing this—by taking actions that create something new rather than just maintain the status quo—we can get enormous power. Power comes naturally in the realm of creation, so an effective way of generating power fast is to simply access this realm.

EXERCISE

Find an area of your life where you're doing things just to maintain the status quo. It could be in the area of your health, the area of your relationships or the area of your career. It's an area where your time and energy is spent on just keeping things the way they are. For instance, you work out so you don't gain weight, or you take your wife out on dates so she doesn't get upset, or you produce just enough results at work so you get reasonably paid and promoted.

 *Innovation is a new combination of already existing elements."*
— BJORN MARTINOFF

Then in the area you've chosen, take an action that creates something new. Run or dance instead of going to the gym. Do something silly with your wife. Ask for a project in your office that's totally foreign to you. The point is: do what it takes to put yourself in the realm of creation rather than in the realm of preservation.

And it's easy to tell when you're in the realm of creation, because the moment you're there, you start feeling excited, you start feeling motivated and you start feeling inspired. In short: you start feeling powerful.

QUESTIONS

1. What areas of your life have become dull and uninspiring?

2. Pick the most important of these areas and check the kinds of actions you've been taking in this area. Have they been actions that create or actions that simply preserve the status quo?

3. What actions that create can you take in this area of your life? List down at least three actions.

4. If you can't think of any actions that create at the moment, then what new dimensions or new contexts can you create in this area of your life? List down at least three new dimensions or contexts.

5. What possible outcomes could arise from you taking on these new actions, dimensions or contexts? Think of at least three possible positive outcomes.

THE POWER OF ACTION

"We are what we repeatedly do. Excellence, therefore, is not an act but a habit."
— ARISTOTLE

2. THE POWER OF ALIGNMENT
BROAD-BASED AGREEMENT

In my experience working with different individuals and organizations from all over the world—from individual executives, small companies and struggling companies to large companies, Fortune 100 companies, and even the world's largest company—I've found that one of the biggest things that gets in the way of success is the absence of alignment. The absence of alignment is one of the greatest detractors from power being applied toward a desired goal.

Alignment is critical in any organization because without broad-based agreement—on goals, strategies and other critical areas—organizations can literally spend a LOT of energy without getting anywhere at all.

Why?

Well, imagine sitting on a boat with two people rowing:

ARTWORK BY RENE TRINIDAD ALDONZA

one person is rowing in one direction and the other person is rowing in the opposite direction. If they're both putting in the same amount of energy, they'll just end up canceling each other's efforts and the boat won't move from its location at all. Or if one person's putting in more energy than the other, the boat will move in his or her direction, but at a much slower pace than they should be getting with the amount of effort they're exerting.

Now imagine this scenario replicated hundreds of times over in the average-sized organization. In the absence of alignment, either there's no progress at all or the progress is severely limited, or it might be going in a different direction than intended.

With alignment, on the other hand, all the individual energies add up and result in a huge amount of momentum. So in cases where a company has clearly established its purpose, its goals and its strategies—and theoretically they're sound—but the company isn't going anywhere, one fruitful area to examine is whether the organization has worked on getting broad-based consensus for its plans.

THE POWER OF ALIGNMENT

> *"Misaligned or even opposing energies and forces are some of the greatest waste and missed opportunities you'll find in organizations."*
> — BJORN MARTINOFF

Having worked with many outsourcing companies (BPOs) I worked with a particular company in Asia that had just been warned by its client in the United States that they were at risk of losing their $11,000,000 account. Let's spell that out: that's eleven million dollars. At the moment I learned about this, the business unit ranked last among its network of peers and its client had given it just two months to turn around the situation. At that point, the predictable future was that the client would pull the account from the unit.

When I started my engagement with the company, I quickly realized that even just in terms of handling the crisis, there was no alignment amongst the top management team. The energies of the leaders were dispersed, their ideas mixed and unclear, the way forward was vague and unchartered. Something was left to be discovered which would make a difference but none of the leaders could say what it was for sure.

After a launching an initial set of diagnostic tools, one of the first things I did with the management team was to help them find alignment and create a common vision, purpose and set of core values.

This wasn't the only intervention I applied, but creating alignment on this broad level provided the foundation for all the other work I had to do with the organization. Without alignment in terms of the direction we were headed, everything else that was going to be said was going to fall on deaf ears. Once all the interventions I proposed were in place, the team went on to become the number two performer in their network and the number one performer in their country—within two months. And none of this would have been possible without an initial alignment of the individual forces.

Alignment applies just as much to the creative field because creative projects are very often collaborative endeavors (at the very least, you still have to please a client—unless your work focuses specifically on producing art). Whether it's writing a novel, designing a website or producing a commercial, all the people involved in a creative project have to be broadly aligned on the outcome to be produced and have to meet periodically to check if their individual efforts remain aligned with the original intention. Maintaining that alignment can take a fair bit of work—especially in fields that are governed by matters of preference and taste—but the additional effort must nevertheless be made.

2.1 VECTOR DYNAMICS

To further demonstrate this, as well as the concept of vector dynamics in leadership, let's look at the following graphics:

Graphic 1:

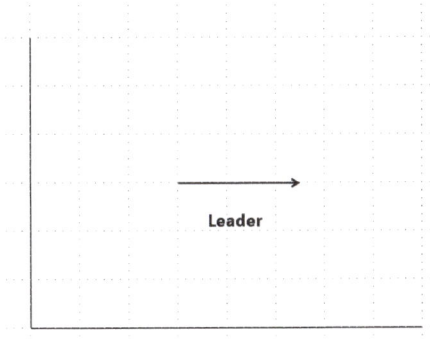

The example in Graphic 1 represents the vector dynamics of a single leader pushing in the direction of her goals or vision. She is a strong leader and pulls forward on a level 2.5. By definition though, you aren't a a leader if you're going it alone, so let's introduce some team members.

Graphic 2:

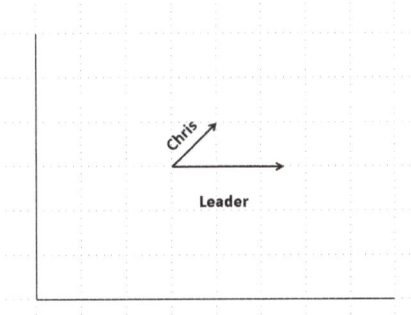

In Graphic 2, Chris is a member of the team. Chris is a professional and appears to be a good team player. Upon further inspection, however, we notice that Chris has an agenda of his own and is not fully aligned with the leader. We realize this must have an impact on the combined performance. The question is how much, and we'll get to see this in the following graphics. In the meantime, let's add a few more team members.

Graphic 3:

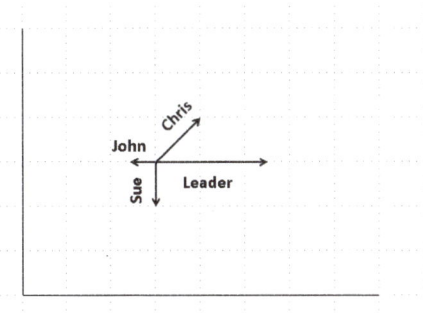

In Graphic 3, we see that our leader now has two additional team members, Sue and John. Sue is in a space where she doesn't really care what she does as long as she brings home a paycheck and is able to pay the bills while John is mildly upset about being where he is as he feels it's just a lateral move and he's not inspired by the direction the leader appears to be heading towards. In fact, John is mildly opposed to where things are heading. Now, you may ask yourself what the effect of these Vector Dynamics are. You'll see this

22 THE POWER OF ALIGNMENT

in the next graphic.

Graphic 4:

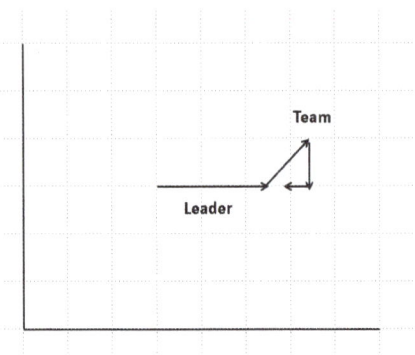

In Graphic 4, we now have all the vectors together. By doing this, we now have a clearer picture of how strongly this team will pull toward the leader's goal. When we connect the starting point to the end point, we now have an image of the actual level of collective effort towards the leader's goal. This will be depicted in Graphic 5.

Graphic 5:

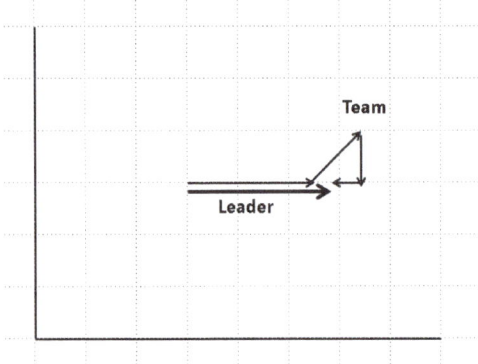

In Graphic 5, the thicker arrow represents the collective push toward the leader's goal (the arrow has been moved slightly lower to improve visibility). This is the sum total of the leader's and the team members' efforts. In this image, you can see that even if the leader has three other people on her team, the combined effort results in an an outcome only marginally greater than that the solitary effort of the leader herself. The next question you will likely ask now is: what is the potential of this specific team if it were aligned in the same direction? Graphic 6 will help show this.

Graphic 6:

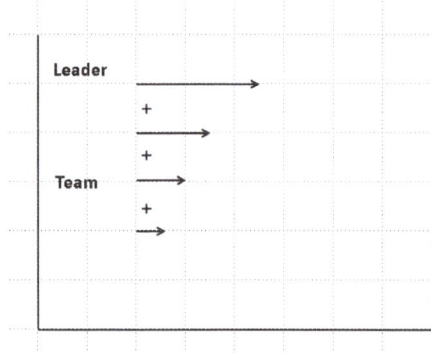

Here we have the invidual vectors shown separately yet in alignment with the leader. What happens when we add them up?

Graphic 7:

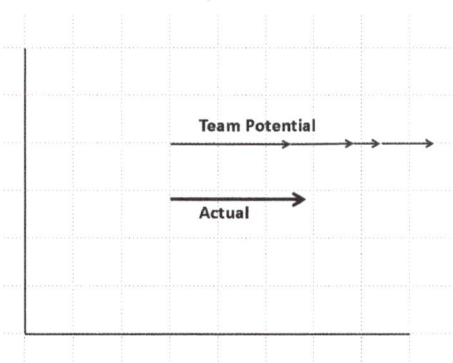

This is what the team potential could look like after full alignment. This does not yet include any increase in motivation due to the alignment.

Truly aligned teams are a force to be reckoned with. This particular team, through alignment, has now approximately doubled its push, energy, power and momentum in the direction of the leader's goal. Another way of looking at it is that it has gained twice as much momentum whereas before it had lost half of its momentum.

This can be quite an eye opening experience for those of us who are leading teams, groups or entire organizations. (Actual results will vary depending on the actual composition and alignment of the team or organization!)

THE POWER OF ALIGNMENT

> *"Just as your car runs more smoothly and requires less energy to go faster and farther when the wheels are in perfect alignment, you and your team perform better when your thoughts, feelings, emotions, goals, actions, and values are in alignment with where you're heading."*
> — BJORN MARTINOFF

The principle of vector dynamics and alignment also applies to individuals, by the way. Even within ourselves, we'll find that we're not completely in alignment with certain goals or targets we have. (Not surprisingly, these are the areas where we experience a lot of struggle or stress in our efforts to succeed.)

Once upon a long, long time ago I was up for a promotion. Part of me wanted to get that job promotion because it meant a lot more money. Another part of me didn't want that job promotion because it also meant a lot more responsibility.

When there are internal conflicts like these, it's literally like having two rowers in the same boat going in completely opposite directions! And that's why even on the level of our individual selves, it's important that we find alignment within.

Any opposing values, beliefs or attitudes will oppose us and ultimately keep us from achieving our goals.

EXERCISE

Find one area in our life where you've experienced a lot of struggle or conflict. It could be your job, a project, one of your relationships, or anything else. Examine that area and identify what elements or values are in conflict.

For example, maybe spending time on Facebook makes you happy, but it also distracts you from your work. Once you've identified the conflicting elements, see how you can create alignment. One option is to create priorities (e.g., work first, Facebook second); another option is to create boundaries (e.g., focus on Facebook only after work hours); yet another option is to eliminate a conflicting element entirely (e.g., delete your Facebook account).

We are what we repeatedly do. Excellence, therefore, is not an act but a habit."— ARISTOTLE

Now, creating alignment isn't easy and it often involves making tough choices. But living without it is even harder. In the absence of alignment, energy is just wasted—and that leaves you with a lot less power to fulfill on what you really want.

QUESTIONS

1. What areas of your life have become full of struggle and conflict?

2. Pick the most important of these areas and ask yourself: Where is alignment missing?

3. Examining your chosen area more closely, ask yourself: What elements exactly are not in alignment? Are there contradictory values? Are there conflicting interests? Are there competing objectives? Note these down with as much detail as you can.

4. What actions can you begin to take to bring alignment where there was previously none? List down at least three actions.

5. What possible outcomes could arise from you taking on these actions? Think of at least three possible positive outcomes.

3. THE POWER OF AUTHENTICITY
COMMUNICATE WHAT'S REAL

ARTWORK BY RENE TRINIDAD ALDONZA

In the chapter on TRUST, I talk about how trust depends on the affinity and affection between people as well as the level and quality of the communication between them.

Now, one of the biggest things that get in the way of people's affinity for and communication between each other is the absence or lack of authenticity.

There are many ways to define authenticity, but in this context, I'm going to define authenticity as our ability to freely express and communicate our experience. Let me say that again: authenticity is our ability to say and share what we truly think and feel with the people around us.

Some of you might be reading this and thinking: Well, I'm a creative person, and creativity comes from being authentic, so this doesn't really apply to me. Or, you might be thinking: It's all good to be authentic, but we can't just go around telling people unpleasant or disappointing or hurtful things right?

On the one hand, both are valid points to make. On the other hand, being authentic in one area of life (like our work life) doesn't necessarily mean being authentic in other areas of our life. In addition, many of us are inauthentic even when there's no risk that what we're saying is unpleasant or disappointing or hurtful. In fact, many of us are inauthentic simply because we want to look good, or we want to fit in, or we don't want to be inconvenienced, possibly even worsen the relationship

So even if it's an outright lie, even if it contradicts what we truly think or how we truly feel, we'll say something just to be polite, just to get off the hook and just to maintain the status quo.

But my question is: how much

THE POWER OF AUTHENTICITY

> "The great majority of us . . . live a life of constant duplicity. Your health is bound to be affected if, day after day, you say the opposite of what you feel, if you grovel before what you dislike, and rejoice at what brings you nothing but misfortune."
>
> — BORIS PASTERNAK

power is there when you hide yourself like that? How much power do you experience every time you misrepresent what you truly think and feel?

I'm willing to bet your answer would be: not very much. Because the fact is, when you're not authentic, it's like putting yourself in a prison. You lose your freedom to express yourself and to be yourself, and your environment ends up dictating who you're going to be and how you're going to behave.

It's as if you're in a prison with the key lost and forever unavailable. Does a person without freedom have power? Does a prisoner have power? Let me tell you there is no power behind bars. A prisoner is someone who has lost all choice, and with the loss of choice you have lost your power. We always have the choice to be authentic and remove the bars around us. Yet when you're hiding behind inauthenticity it's like you're putting yourself behind bars. You have effectively imprisoned yourself and given away your power. You have become too afraid to be real. It is fear, and not politeness and not culture, that has people be inauthentic and unreal.

In short, you lose a huge amount of power.

Besides the loss of power you personally experience when you're being inauthentic, there's also the loss of affinity, communication and trust between you and the other person.

Why?

Because if you're not being honest with the other person, how can you genuinely expect them to be honest with you? Whenever one party in a relationship starts being inauthentic, it's only a matter of time before the other party starts being inauthentic too. Before long, the relationship will begin to deteriorate—if not fall apart altogether. The relationship will go into a downward spiral.

On the other hand, it only takes one party being authentic for the other party to start being authentic too. Haven't you noticed that in your relationships, especially at the beginning of your friendships? Someone who was once just an acquaintance suddenly shares something very intimate about themselves, and the next thing you know, you're telling them some pretty intimate details about your life too. That's when the relationship shifts from a mere acquaintance to a real friendship.

Sometimes, the initiative to share something more personal comes from you. Regardless of who takes the initiative, my point is that once someone in the relationship makes the effort to be authentic, it usually inspires or encourages the other party to be authentic as well. And within that relationship, there's affinity, there's communication, there's trust and there's power.

EXPONENTIAL POWER FOR CREATIVE DESIGN PROFESSIONALS HANDBOOK

EXERCISE

Go back into your life and identify at least one relationship where there's been a loss or lack of affinity, communication and trust coming from an absence of authenticity. It could be with your mother-in-law (whom you're always trying to please), or it could be with your boss (whom you're always trying to impress), or it could be with your spouse (whom you're always trying to reassure). The point is: find someone in your life with whom you haven't been completely honest. Maybe you didn't lie to them, but you didn't tell them everything either.

Now here's the exercise: tell this person that you haven't been honest with them and tell them why you were afraid of being honest with them. Say what you need to say without holding anything back (you might need to read the chapter on COURAGE before you do this!). Be fully authentic with this person, whoever he or she is—and then see what it provides: for you, for the other person, and for the relationship itself.

Just one note about this exercise: being authentic with someone doesn't mean hurting them or insulting them. There is a way of expressing what's genuinely there for you, if it's unpleasant, without being hurtful or offensive—and that's by telling the other person that what you're sharing with them is your experience of a particular action rather than an assessment of who they really are.

For example, instead of saying "You're mean and you belittle me all the time," you can say "Every time you say I can't do something, it hurts me and makes me feel incapable." By pointing to a specific action and its specific impact on you, the other person gets that it's not who they are that's being attacked, like there's something wrong with them, but that there are certain things they do that aren't workable for you.

Doing this can be tricky at first since we're more used to accusing people in general rather than pinpointing specific actions, but it makes a HUGE difference in how receptive people will be to what you're communicating to them.

And, I assure you that however it turns out, just making the enormous effort required in being authentic will already increase your level of power.

"Authenticity is the alignment of head, mouth, heart, and feet - thinking, saying, feeling, and doing the same thing - consistently. This builds trust, and followers love leaders they can trust."
— *LANCE SECRETAN*

QUESTIONS

1. Which relationships in your life have become marked by concealment, evasion or half-truths? The latter don't need to be very dramatic—it can be as simple as consistently telling someone that you're feeling great even when you really don't feel fine.

2. Pick the most important of these relationships and ask yourself: What it's like for you in this relationship? Does it contribute positively to your experience of life or negatively?

3. What actions can you take to begin restoring authenticity in this relationship? List down at least three actions.

4. What possible outcomes could arise from you taking on these actions? Think of at least three possible positive outcomes.

5. What do you think being authentic will provide for the other person in the relationship? Think of at least three possible benefits for the other person!

4. THE POWER OF BELIEF
SHAPING REALITY

People often think that the only basis for a belief is how true something is in reality. That is, we should only believe in things whose truth we can demonstrate (hence the saying "to see is to believe").

But what people don't realize is that belief isn't just something that results from something being true. In fact, in many cases, it's our belief that causes something to be true.

Said another way, our beliefs don't necessarily need to depend on reality, because the power of our belief can actually shape and produce reality. Many of the things we now take for granted as real—like the possibility of flight or the possibility of space travel—became real only because of the power of belief. People in the creative fields understand this truth on a gut level (at least in the area of their work) because unless they believe that they can create something where previously nothing had existed—whether it be a book, a painting or a film—they would simply be unable to do their jobs!

The power of belief is really important to get because by not understanding this, people overlook or underestimate belief as a tool they can use to shape their lives. Worse, they end up unconsciously using their beliefs in ways that even set them back!

The most classic example of an unproductive or even damaging belief is the belief that we're not good enough. A belief like this prevents people from exploring opportunities, and when people don't explore, they

ARTWORK BY RENE TRINIDAD ALDONZA

THE POWER OF BELIEF

> "Believe nothing, no matter where you read it or who said it, not even if I have said it, unless it agrees with your own reason and your own common sense."
> — THE BUDDHA

can't learn, and when they can't learn, they certainly can't get good at something. Hence, this is a reality-producing belief rather than a reality-dependent belief. (This goes for most of the beliefs we have of ourselves and of other people, by the way!)

An example of this from my own life is a belief I used to have that I couldn't speak in front of groups of people. I had lots of evidence for this belief, including the fact that I would stutter whenever I was talking to more than one person. So, because I believed that I couldn't talk to big groups (or even just small groups for that matter), I never attempted. Because I never gave it a shot, I never got speaking opportunities—which only further reinforced my belief that I couldn't talk in front of groups of people. You get the picture.

I finally got to address my belief when I pinpointed its origin. My belief that I couldn't talk to groups of people started when I was in sixth grade. During a class exercise where we were asked to list down topics that we wanted to learn about, I wrote down wanting to study the battle strategies of Julius Caesar. When my classmates heard about what I wrote, they started laughing! And in that moment, I decided that the things that interested Me didn't interest other people and that they therefore didn't want to listen to anything I had to say. My fear of talking to groups of people therefore came from my childhood belief that people didn't want to listen to anything I had to say!

When I realized this, I got clear that my inability to speak in front of people was the result of a childhood belief that wasn't even based on anything accurate. Because my classmates laughed when they found out that I wanted to study Julius Caesar, I took their laughter to mean that:

(1) they weren't interested in what I was interested in;
(2) no one else could possibly be interested in what I was interested in; and
(3) no one could possibly want to listen to me.

But the facts are:

(1) my classmates could have laughed for other reasons besides being disinterested;
(2) many people are interested in Julius Caesar (or how else could the History Channel be so popular?); and
(3) even if other people don't share my interest in Julius Caesar, it doesn't mean that they wouldn't be interested in listening to me.

When I finally let go of my childhood belief, the alteration in my ability to speak in front of people was just amazing. Now, I speak regularly to groups of 400 to 500 people. I don't stutter anymore, I enjoy myself immensely and my audience gets enormous value from what I have to say. That's a real-life example of how belief is shaping reality.

Look at it this way: whatever you believe about yourself, you're right. If you believe you can make it, you're right. If you believe you can't make

THE POWER OF BELIEF

it, you're also right. If the Wright brothers had believed that flight was impossible for human beings, they would never have invented the world's first successful airplane and they would have ended up being right.

So my question to you is: Which of your beliefs about yourself will serve you better? Is it the belief that you can't do something or the belief that you can do something?

I'm willing to bet on what your answer will be.

> "Be patient, your blessings and dreams are coming into your life! Just keep believing!"
> — *CASSANDRA MANUEL FRANSIER*

THE POWER OF BELIEF

■ EXERCISE

> "Keep your dreams alive. Understand to achieve anything requires faith and belief in yourself, vision, hard work, determination, and dedication. Remember all things are possible for those who believe."
> — GAIL DEVERS

Choose one thing in your life that you've always said you couldn't do. It can be a simple thing like dancing or a complicated thing like flying an airplane. Whatever it is, just do it.

In some cases, you'll need to take lessons. But whatever you end up doing, I only have one instruction: you really have to let go of your belief that you can't do it.

This is absolutely important, because if you don't let go of that belief, all your efforts will be doomed. You'll ignore or downplay your accomplishments and you'll exaggerate your failings and mistakes. At some point, you'll give up altogether—and it's the giving up that will make your belief that you can't do it true.

So keep believing that you can do it and keep going for it. I promise you, you'll be surprised at what you can actually accomplish once you let go of all of your beliefs to the contrary.

QUESTIONS

1. In what areas of your life do you find yourself held back or stuck?

2. Pick the most important of these areas and ask yourself: What beliefs do you have about yourself in this area?

3. Working with the same area, ask yourself: What beliefs do you have about others in this area?

4. Still working with the same area, ask yourself: What beliefs do you have about your circumstances in this area?

5. Finally, ask yourself: Have any of the beliefs you've listed down contributed to your lack of progress or success in this area? Answer honestly.

5. THE POWER OF CHOICE

OPERATES BEYOND THE LEVEL OF THE TANGIBLE

People often believe that the exercise of choice is limited to areas where the options or possibilities are tangible or concrete, and that when there's only one such option or possibility available, then they don't have a choice.

For example, people think that if the only way for them to pay a debt is to take on a job that they dislike, they will often say afterwards that they took the job because they "didn't have a choice."

But choice is a capacity that operates on many different levels—and the level of the tangible or concrete choice is just one of the lowest. The Austrian psychiatrist Viktor Frankl, one of the few survivors of the Nazi concentration camps and the inventor of logotherapy, once said: "Everything can be taken from a man but one thing; the last of the human freedoms—to choose one's

ARTWORK BY RENE TRINIDAD ALDONZA

attitude in any given set of circumstances, to choose one's own way."

This is absolutely critical because there are many instances in life where we find ourselves without choices at the tangible or concrete level. But the lack of choice on this level doesn't need to lead to a loss of power on our part. Until the very last moment, like Frankl said, we will always have the power of choice—even if it's a power that will be limited to our choice of attitude alone.

It might be easy to belittle the value of this, but our choice of attitude is enormously powerful. For Frankl, his steadfast belief in the value of life in the face of all the horrors that surrounded him during the Holocaust made all the difference in his ability to survive—and he observed that it was the same case with other survivors as well. Prisoners that gave in to their resignation, on the other hand, literally died.

It's not likely that we'll face circumstances similar to Frankl's, and we're very lucky in this regard, but it doesn't mean that we can't benefit from the wisdom he gained from his experiences.

In my life, I've experienced the power of choice in the

THE POWER OF CHOICE

> "You always do what you want to do. This is true with every act. You may say that you had to do something, or that you were forced to, but actually, whatever you do, you do by choice. Only you have the power to choose for yourself."
>
> — W. CLEMENT STONE

area of my relationship with my wife. See, in the same way that you have a choice with regard to your attitude, as Frankl pointed out, you also have a choice with regard to the things on which you focus. (You might want read the chapter on FOCUS after this, if you haven't read it already).

If you look at your own relationships, particularly the romantic ones, you'll notice that in the beginning, everything's just perfect: the other person never does anything wrong. Then as time goes on and the relationship matures, suddenly the other person starts doing all kinds of things—undesirable things—that they never used to do before.

But the fact is, the other person never changed. It's just that at the beginning of the relationship, our focus is on all the things that we find desirable about the other person. All the other undesirable things are already there—we just never pay them any attention! But as the relationship progresses, our focus slowly expands to include everything that the other person does. So it's not that they suddenly start doing things that we don't like, rather, it's that we start noticing these things for the first time.

And this is where choice enters the picture, because what we focus on is also a matter of choice. When our relationships begin to sour, in many cases it's because we've begun to focus only on the things that we find undesirable. Just choosing to adjust our focus can have a huge impact on the quality of our relationships.

Choosing what to focus on was precisely what altered my relationship with my wife. When I chose to focus once again on what was great about her and what was great about our relationship, I went from wanting to complain all the time to being grateful—in just a few seconds! The shift was just amazing.

One area where creative people often find themselves seemingly bereft of the power of choice is the area of what the client wants. Very often, a creative professional can find himself or herself struggling to reconcile what the client wants with what he or she feels should be done on an artistic level. Then a sense of frustration kicks in, accompanied by an internal conversation that starts along the lines of "I don't have a choice, it's what the client wants…"

If this happens to you, consider that you do have a choice: it just operates on a slightly different level. Maybe you can't choose what the client wants, but you can certainly choose what to focus on in the situation (such as the fact that you have a client who's willing to pay for your work!).

The point is: choice gives us power, and because, as Frankl insists, we will always have a level of choice, then the good news is that we will always have a level of power.

EXERCISE

Find an area of your life that's disempowered you because you've always felt that you "didn't have a choice" in that area. Then ask yourself: what has your sense of disempowerment, bitterness, disappointment, frustration and resentment in that area actually provided for you? Has it made a positive difference? Or did it just make things much harder for you?

If you find that your attitude or focus in this area has only made things worse, consider that your attitude or focus is actually a choice—and that you have a very real power to choose something else more empowering. (For pointers on how to generate a more empowering attitude, you can refer to the chapters on INSPIRATION and INTERPRETATION.)

QUESTIONS

1. In what areas of your life do you feel like you have to do things because "you don't have a choice?"

2. Pick the most important of these areas and ask yourself: On what level does the perceived absence of choice actually occur? Is it on the tangible level or on the intangible level?

3. Working with the same area, what's the impact on you from believing that you don't have a choice in this area of your life?

4. Still working with the same area, what's the choice you can create for yourself on this level or on the more intangible level?

5. What does creating choice in this area provide for you? List at least three possible benefits.

"It is our choices that show what we truly are, far more than our abilities."
— J.K. ROWLING

6. THE POWER OF COMMITMENT
GOING RIGHT AHEAD AND DOING SOMETHING

Commitment is an over-used word—and one that's often misunderstood. One of the ways people misunderstand commitment is by associating it with the word "try." People believe that to be committed means to try very hard in the area of one's commitment.

On the contrary, there's nothing more non-committal than the very notion of trying. One way I demonstrate this in my capacity as an executive coach is to have my clients do the following exercise:

First, I'll put a pen in front of my client. Then I'll tell him or her that I'm going to ask them to do two very different things. The first thing I'll ask them to do is to "pick up the pen"—which they'll usually do without any difficulty.

Then I'll ask them to "try to pick up the pen"—and this is where things get complicated. Most of my clients will go

ARTWORK BY RENE TRINIDAD ALDONZA

right ahead and pick up the pen. Then I'll shake my head and remind them that I told them at the start that they were to do two different things, the first of which was to "pick up the pen" and the second of which was to "try to pick up the pen."

At this point, most of them will think for a few seconds, and then go right ahead and pick up the pen. Then I'll remind them once again that

that's not what I asked them to do. By this time, a few will look perplexed while a lot will look downright annoyed. Then for every instance afterwards that they'll pick up the pen, I'll just tell them all over again that the instruction was to "try to pick up the pen."

Some of my clients get this really fast while others take several attempts. Done correctly, "trying" will look

> "Unless commitment is made there are only promises and hopes; but no plans."
> — *PETER DRUCKER*

something like this: my client will have his or her hand hovering in the air, but will never actually touch the pen. Or, they'll be touching the pen, but they'll never actually pick it up.

You get the picture. It's the same in any creative endeavor after all. You either write or you don't write. You either paint or you don't paint. You either take photographs or you don't take photographs. There's no point in between. But just for the sake of demonstrating a point, try this exercise for yourself (pun not intended). You'll notice that when you're "trying" to pick up the pen, it feels as if one set of muscles is pulling in one direction and another set of muscles is pulling in the opposite direction. It requires twice the effort to "try" to do something and it also wastes a lot of time.

This is what I mean when I say that trying is actually very non-committal. Real commitment is just going right ahead and doing something.

Most people actually get this. For instance, have you noticed that when someone asks you to do something you don't want to do, and you don't want to say no outright, you often tell them that you're going to "try"? It's one strategy we've learned in order to be politely non-committal. In general, when we use the word "try," we use it in relation to areas where we're not very sure we'll actually succeed.

Children, on the other hand, don't try (they haven't learned the strategy yet). They go right ahead and do things. When they fail, they learn from the experience and go at it again. If you've ever watched a toddler learning to walk, you'll know what I mean.

THE POWER OF COMMITMENT

■ EXERCISE

When you catch yourself saying "I'll try" in an area that matters to you, stop yourself and make a commitment instead. You can do this by simply saying when you'll get the task done. Declaring a deadline is enormously effective (as creative professionals will know!) because otherwise, you'll just put off doing your commitment to "someday" (and if you've noticed, "someday" never appears on any calendar!). Stating a place is helpful too.

In my observation, commitments turn into reality much faster whenever a date and a place are attached to their fulfillment. Giving a commitment without stating when and where you'll get it done is like inviting someone to a party without telling them what time it'll start and where it'll be held.

So when a client asks me if I can send a proposal as soon as possible, instead of saying "I'll try," I'll say: "You'll have it on your desk by ten o'clock tomorrow." Or if I am busy that day I will ask them by what day they'd like to have it on their desk. By saying this to my client I have effectively engaged them as an observer who will clearly be able to tell whether I am keeping my word or not. By doing so I make sure I keep my commitment and also remain in integrity with my word.

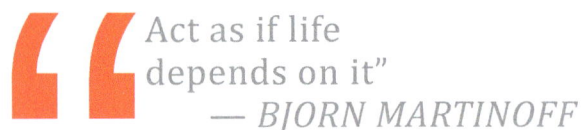

> "Act as if life depends on it"
> — BJORN MARTINOFF

Committing myself in this way has me do everything I can to fulfill the commitment—which vastly increases my power in getting things done—because for one reason or another, it seems easier to keep our commitments to others than to ourselves.

Want to create an even greater level of commitment for yourself? Just do this: Pretend your life or the life of someone dear to you depends on it. It is amazing what we can accomplish when life depends on it.

QUESTIONS

1. In what areas of your life do you find yourself using the word "try" a lot?

2. Pick the most important of the above areas and ask yourself: Are you effective in this area of your life?

3. Working with the same area, ask yourself: What's the concrete impact of my being non-committal in this area?

4. Still working with the same area, ask yourself: What commitment can I take on in this area? This can mean finally committing to working on this area, or, it can mean committing to NOT working on this area altogether. Either way, there's a clear commitment.

5. Having taken on a clear commitment (whatever it happens to be), what's there for you right now?

7. THE POWER OF CONTRIBUTION

INCLUDE THE WELFARE OF OTHERS

One of the least intuitive ways of generating power for yourself lies in being a contribution to other people. I'll say that again: one of the most effective ways you'll ever discover of empowering yourself lies in empowering others. Nothing is more fulfilling and nothing else will open more flood gates to success. When you're contributing to others, when you're making a difference, it's as if you are on the side of good—the side of God.

Now, I'm not saying this coming from the logic that the good that you do will always find its way back to you in the way you expect it to. The good you do will bounce back to you eventually, though rarely in the exact way you expect it. However what you can expect is that it will and that it does.

This truth is what some call karma.

That karma even exists may be difficult to get or swallow. But it certainly can be observed and experienced. Let me explain.

Whenever I coach an executive who's nervous before making a big presentation, I usually ask him or her a very simple question: "At this very moment, what are you focusing on?"

I usually get the some of the following answers:

"I'm wondering about how I look."

"I'm worrying about how prepared I am."

"I'm thinking about what they'll think."

"I'm hoping that I'm not going to make a mistake."

"I'm wondering if my pants are zipped."

ARTWORK BY RENE TRINIDAD ALDONZA

"I'm worrying that I'm sweating too much."

If you look at all the answers above, you'll realize that they have one thing in common—which is that in all cases, the person is focusing on himself or herself. Whenever a client of mine starts focusing inwards rather than outwards, that's when their nervousness begins.

The same thing happens

THE POWER OF CONTRIBUTION

to me too. Whenever I focus on myself during a presentation—either worrying about my appearance or worrying about my performance—that's when I usually start getting nervous and uncertain. My voice will start trembling. I'll start having difficulties looking people in the eye. I'll start losing my connection to the audience. I'll start losing my train of thought.

Then when I finally notice what's going on with me, I'll stop and ask myself the question that my friend Anthony Robbins always likes to ask: "What are you focusing on, Bjorn?"

And when I am nervous or anxious the answer will always be the same: "I'm focusing on myself."

But when I start focusing on the people in front of me rather than on myself, there's an immediate and palpable shift in my level of power. When my concern shifts from am I doing it right to what will make a difference for my audience, the anxiety fades, the nervousness stops and the uncertainty disappears. From that point onwards, the only thing that's occupying me is how to make a difference for my audience—there's literally no room to be worrying about anything else, least of all myself.

Now this can be counterintuitive for a lot of people. It seems to make more sense for us to focus on ourselves if we want to increase our power. But paradoxically, it's when we focus on others with an intention to be a contribution to them that we're actually at our most powerful.

That's why it's not a coincidence that the most powerful people in history and in the world are the people who've made the biggest difference in other people's lives. Think about Nelson Mandela, the Buddha, Christ, Gandhi, Martin Luther King, Jr., Mother Teresa and Princess Diana. They were enormously powerful people—and their lives were focused completely on others. Now let me talk about what I mentioned earlier: which is that the good that we do for others eventually finds its way back to us.

When I was younger, my life was really just about me. I didn't care about anyone or anything else. I did pretty okay—but I was never as successful as I wanted to be. Then for various reasons

> "Act as if what you do makes a difference. It does."
> — W.ILLIAM JAMES

which I won't recount here, I eventually shifted my focus to include the welfare of other people around me.

And when I did, I noticed the most surprising thing: my success started to take off. Business was easier, achievement came faster, and I felt more fulfilled, more grateful and more joyful.

Being a contribution allowed me to increase my level of achievement, and at the same time, a higher level of achievement allowed me to make even bigger contributions to others and my charities. The more I gave, the more I grew; and the more I grew, the more I was able to give. I gave away advice, money and time—and I got them all back tenfold and in various ways.

A person though can't genuinely be a contribution if all they're after is getting something back.

The moral law of the universe will have you reap whatever it is you've sown. If you give,

46 THE POWER OF CONTRIBUTION

you will eventually receive. It's that simple. Just don't expect to receive something from the same direction that you gave, because I've found that the universe doesn't necessarily work that way. Sometimes, you can find your contribution coming back to you in completely unexpected—but always welcome—ways.

Being a contribution requires a lot of faith and courage though. (You might want to read the chapters on COURAGE and FAITH if you haven't done so already.) There are times in our lives when it's just difficult to be generous!

For example, when I first started tithing, which is the practice of giving ten percent of one's income as a contribution to charities, it was incredibly hard. To give that much income away when I didn't always have enough food in the refrigerator was tough.

But something always came through, and since I began tithing, my income has actually tripled (and even quadrupled) at times. That's the power of contribution.

But, you may say, Bjorn, I really don't have any money. Even if you're not in a position to give money, you can always be a contribution in other ways. Besides tithing, for instance, I also support a non-profit organization in the Philippines that tutors underprivileged and academically challenged children. I don't just provide financial assistance to the organization—I also provide coaching and mentoring to its founder.

The point is: there are so many ways that you can be a contribution—and all you need is yourself and some time, and nothing else.

The next time you're involved in a creative project and you're out of ideas and out of inspiration, try asking yourself: what's the difference I can make in this project? See if asking yourself that question makes a difference for you.

THE POWER OF CONTRIBUTION

■ EXERCISE

> "Change your focus, from making money to serving more people. Serving more people makes the money come in."
> — ROBERT KIYOSAKI

Next time you're about to do something in an area where you don't have much confidence, ask yourself: "What can I do at this moment that will make a difference for the other people involved?"

Once you come up with something, focus all your attention on it for the rest of the time—and then see what a difference that makes for you and your level of power and confidence.

QUESTIONS

1. In what areas of your life ddo you feel like you don't have enough of something, whether that's time, skill, money or knowledge?

2. What do you think it would provide for you if you practiced being a contribution in these areas instead of giving in to the feelings of lack?

3. What daily practice can you set for yourself to create a habit of contributing?

4. What daily practice can you create in the area of your life that you selected above?

5. Having taken on a clear commitment (whatever it happens to be), what's there for you right now?

8. THE POWER OF COURAGE
ACTING IN THE PRESENCE OF FEAR

ARTWORK BY RENE TRINIDAD ALDONZA

It doesn't take any courage to walk through your apartment door. But it's a different story when that same door is engulfed in flames.

People quite often think of courage as the absence of fear. But courage is not the absence of fear. Rather, courage is acting in the presence of fear.

Let me say that again: courage is not the absence of fear, but the ability to act in the presence of fear. Your ability to act in spite of your fear is what courage is.

Why people often misunderstand courage is because people often misunderstand fear. In our culture, it's very easy to belittle fear. The popular view is that fear holds us back and gets in our way and it's therefore best to get rid of our fear (hence the slogan "No fear" that shows up on many bumper stickers and t-shirts).

But fear plays an important role in our lives by acting as a signal that we perceive a threat to our physical or psychological well-being. Without the presence of fear to warn us, we would likely act in ways that would jeopardize our safety, like tiptoeing on cliff edges, eating unfamiliar fruits or manhandling snakes. So fear is useful and valuable and our lives would be harder and literally more dangerous without its presence.

What makes fear a little tricky is that it doesn't discriminate between different kinds of threats. You will have the same sensations and symptoms of fear facing a black widow spider and thinking of speaking in public (if that happens to be one of your fears). In the first instance, the fear is completely valid and it would be wise to walk away carefully and call an emergency hotline if you got bitten. In the second instance, the fear is completely counterproductive—especially when speaking in public will further your goals and intentions.

Unfortunately, most of the fears we have in our lives are like the second kind: completely counterproductive. This is why in the book, The Teachings of Don Juan, Don Juan tells the book's author Carlos Castañeda that fear is the first of our "four natural enemies" and therefore the first enemy we have to overcome.

This is where courage enters the picture. Courage is about taking action, not because fear is absent, but because we recognize that giving in to the particular fear we're feeling is counterproductive to our goals and intentions.

In my case, the desire to be courageous arose when I was very young. When I was just a little boy, I was scared of heights. My parents used to take me to the Stuttgart Television Tower, and by the time I was two meters away from the railing, I'd already by flat on the ground from terror. My father called me a coward for a long time because of this, and that triggered my desire to overcome fear.

Fortunately enough for me, I found good coaches and mentors later on in my life, and with their guidance, I started doing things that used to terrify me—starting with small and even silly things. For instance, have you ever noticed that when people enter an elevator, they start staring at the buttons like they're the most fascinating things in the world? No one says anything and no one looks at any other person in the eye.

So one small exercise I took on was to talk to people in elevators—even if just for a few minutes. At some point, I even started having fun! The more courage I found, the more outrageous I got. I'd start telling people entering the elevator things like "Welcome aboard the Starship Enterprise!"

And just this small exercise allowed me to overcome a fear of talking to strangers. The thing about overcoming a fear is that the first step is always the hardest—even if the first step doesn't look particularly scary.

> *Feel the fear and do it anyways."*
>
> — SUSAN JEFFERS

But the great thing is that every small step we take to overcome a fear slowly expands the range of our comfort zone. Once we've overcome one small fear, we've overcome it forever and we're ready to take the next small step. We keep pushing the edge of our fear this way: taking one small step further, then another small step further, and so on and so forth, until before we know it, our whole comfort zone has expanded beyond what we ever thought was possible.

The other great thing about conquering fear is that overcoming a fear in one area of life seems to have an impact on our ability to overcome fears in other areas of life.

I usually put it this way: cultivating our courage is like blowing up a balloon—it's the whole thing that expands and not just one region. If we keep blowing up the balloon, it'll get bigger and bigger, until one day it'll pop.

THE POWER OF COURAGE   51

When that day comes, you'll find that you really have no fear anymore (or at least no inauthentic fear). That's when you'll know that you've practiced courage enough times to vanquish that first natural enemy.

You don't even have to start small. If courage is exercised whenever fear is present, then the greatest number of opportunities to practice courage can be found in the areas where there is the most amount of fear to face: namely, the areas of our For people in the creative professions, one such aspiration could be going freelance—finally working without the safety net of a bigger organization. For others, it could be the dream of undertaking their heart project—finally writing that book, or shooting that film, or mounting that exhibit that they'd wanted to do since they were a child (and that was probably the reason they became a creative professional to begin with!).

It's in these areas where we go after what we want the most that we have the most fear, apprehension and anxiety. (That's why when people tell me that they have no fear, I'm left wondering if they truly have no fear, or, if they're simply not going after what they really want.) It's these areas that present the most valuable opportunities—and offer the greatest rewards—in cultivating courage.

> "Courage is resistance to fear, mastery of fear not absence of fear."
> — *MARK TWAIN*

EXERCISE

> ""Do the thing you fear the most and the death of fear is certain."
> — MARK TWAIN

Commit to take on a small act of courage every day. I don't mean "do something stupid or reckless" or "put your life in danger." I mean taking action in areas where your fear is counterproductive—whether it's a small area or a big area.

So ask someone out. Say hello to a stranger in the elevator. Wear the shoes you always thought you'd never pull of wearing. Tell your mother and father you love them. Use every available opportunity to practice courage. By doing so, you cultivate it much faster as a habit, which will then allow you to use it for the really scary things in life (like finally asking someone to marry you our or setting up your own business or buying your dream home even though the payment is more than half of your monthly paycheck).

QUESTIONS

1. In what areas of your life do you find yourself held back by fear?

2. Select one area and examine the fear involved. Is the fear caused by an actual physical threat or by a social threat to your ego?

3. What's been the impact of giving in to fear in this area of your life?

4. What small step can you take in this area to begin confronting your fear?

5. What would it provide for you if you moved ahead in that area and took action in spite of your fear?

> "Do the thing you fear the most and the death of fear is certain."
> — *MARK TWAIN*

9. THE POWER OF DETACHMENT
THE ABILITY TO LET GO

People typically think of detachment as the opposite of achievement, determination or drive. That is, people tend to believe that if you're detached, you've given up on the idea of goals as a whole and that you've stopped going after them or even setting them altogether!

However, this is not what I mean by detachment. Here, I define detachment as the ability to let go of our attachment to the results of our efforts.

Let me repeat that: detachment is the ability to let go of our attachment to the results of our efforts. It is not letting go of making an effort altogether.

Contrary to what many people think, detachment is actually crucial to achievement, determination and drive.

ARTWORK BY RENE TRINIDAD ALDONZA

Why?

Because if you're emotionally attached to a particular outcome, it is the fear of the emotion we will feel IF we fail that can stop us in our tracks before we even get started.

If you're emotionally attached to a specific way the outcome should look like, you're likely to get upset if that exact outcome isn't achieved. Getting upset will then only further block your progress by diverting your attention and energy away from the actions that could put you back on the path towards your goal. Emotional detachment is therefore essential in maintaining

THE POWER OF DETACHMENT

the focus and peace of mind that are necessary for accomplishment of any kind. This can sound paradoxical to commitment, and in some ways it is, but try this on to see how it feels before you judge.

Detachment can even be applied not just to the goals we seek, but to the means that we employ in achieving those goals. Very often, we're attached to a particular way of accomplishing things—ways that have worked for us effectively in the past or we've seen work effectively for others.

Many times though, our preconceived notions of what's effective can often lead to the lack of results or even an undesirable result altogether! Hence, detachment in this area means a willingness to let go of our attachment to how things should get done, or have always been done.

This detachment is especially vital in creative lines of work, for many different reasons. Outcomes are innately difficult to predict when it comes to artistic endeavors because inspiration evolves, or clients change their minds, or team mates do something or come up with something completely unexpected. Detachment allows a creative professional to follow the flow of inspiration, to adapt to changing requirements and to integrate rather than be taken aback by new developments.

I learned detachment the hard way in my personal life—especially in the area of romantic relationships. For the longest time, I wanted to date a specific kind of girl, and my attachment to my criteria probably led me to miss going out with women who may have been a better match for me.

For instance, the first time I started dating after a long time of being single, I thought I might try to go out with an Italian girl. Sure enough, I met one within seven weeks, but my attachment to "dating an Italian girl" led me to overlook other things that were frankly more important in making a relationship last. So the Italian girl and I didn't last more than a couple of dates.

This type of relationship eventually became a pattern because I didn't understand what detachment meant. What I ended up doing again and again was to make my list of criteria even

> "He who would be serene and pure needs but one thing, detachment."
> — *MEISTER ECKHART*

longer—which simply meant expanding the number of things to which I was attached.

After the Italian girl, for instance, I drew up a new list of attributes I wanted in an ideal mate that was a fully typed up two pages long. Again, the girl described on the list showed up in a few weeks, and again, the relationship didn't last. The relationship didn't last because on my two page list, I'd somehow forgotten to include two very important requirements: (1) she should be geographically accessible; and (2) she be monogamous. Well, the girl that showed up didn't meet either requirement. So obviously the relationship didn't work out. I could have easily overcome the geographical challenge, but the thing about her seeing more than one guy at a time didn't sit quite so well with me.

After that relationship ended another two years went by

56 THE POWER OF DETACHMENT

and I finally decided to create another list, and this time I was going to make sure that I included everything that I could possibly think of that was important. So when I was finished I had written up a list eight pages long.

I emailed it to my dear brother and highly respected friend Steve Miller in California to take a look at. His immediate response: "You're crazy. This person does NOT exist!"

I thought: Well, I've made all that effort, so I might as well see what happens.

And sure enough, a woman showed up again in about eight weeks or so. She covered about 96 to 98 percent of my list, and even though we had a slow start, we hit it off quite well and eventually got engaged. But again it wasn't more than a few months into the relationship that I realized that I had forgotten something that I should have included in my list. The item I forgot on my list was that her parents should like me too. Duh!

The relationship didn't last because once again, I'd forgotten to include something important on my list, which was that the woman's parents should like me as well.

Again much time went by after that happened. I was confused, I didn't know whether to be happy that the universe had fulfilled my list and given me what I wanted or to be upset because even though I had gotten what I wanted it didn't work out. At the same time as all that was happening, everything else also seemed to be falling apart in my life. My finances went berserk, I lost my job, and a theft at work left me depleted of the tools of my trade. Something inside me told me it was all good though because it was time to move on and start a new chapter in my life.

I started that new chapter in early 2005 by moving from Los Angeles to Asia. I was scheduled to be in Manila, Philippines, in May for a project and was planning to travel to India after to spend some time in an ashram or two.

Life, it turns out, always has surprises in store for you and usually when you least expect it. I had this feeling that something or someone special would come into my life on this trip but I had no idea as to when or where.

True enough, while I was in Manila, an acquaintance suggested that I attend this particular weekend seminar. On the evening before it was scheduled to start, I began contemplating my life, the upcoming seminar and my planned trip to India. Again, there was that sense that something special was going to happen—possibly while I was attending the weekend seminar.

Now, many times in my life, I had spoken to my angels. Did you know that each of us has at least two angels? That night, I decided to talk to my angels and ask for their help. Because while I had made a list on several occasions detailing what I wanted in a life partner, and while I had met women who nearly perfectly matched my list each time, none of the relationships ever worked out. Something wasn't working, and I needed help. Eventually it came to me. I realized that I thought I knew best. I had believed that what was on my list was what was best for me. But was it really? Reality had shown that it wasn't just important what was on the list—it was also very important what was left out of the list.

At that point, I decided to

THE POWER OF DETACHMENT

speak to God directly. And this is what I remember saying to him:

Dear God, you have always given me what I wrote down and wanted. Every time you gave me what was on my list and I am grateful for that. However, in the process I've learned that I always seem to forget to ask for that one additional thing. The list always seems incomplete and I realize now that I don't know how to make a complete list for something as important as a life partner. God, you know me perfectly. You know what I want and you also know what's best for me. I've been making these lists based on my own limited perspective, and none of them have worked because there's always something I end up forgetting or not realizing! So given that you have known me since my creation and know what I want and that you know what's best for me, please give me that which is best for me in a life partner—possibly keeping my list in mind. Thank you. And guess what happened next. The very next day, I met Vicki—the woman who is now my wife and the mother of my children.

Now, you don't have to be a believer for this principle to work. Whether you believe in a God or not and whether you pray to a God or not, what's critical is learning how to be detached, to let God (or the universe!) handle the rest and have faith that the right thing is going to happen.

This is what I call detachment. It is letting go of the emotional attachment to a specific outcome. Because when you want a specific outcome very badly, you might actually miss better opportunities that are staring you in the face or coming your way. Or when you're attached to doing things in a very specific way, you might miss opportunities for accomplishing your objectives in faster or more fulfilling ways. It's important to have intentions and it's important to be specific about your intentions— the key is in not getting emotionally attached to a specific outcome even when you're committed to it.

In the end my wife Vicki 'only' matched 75 percent of the items on my list, but as of 2012 we've been together for seven years and we now have four beautiful children. Of course, detachment is much easier said than done. A few years ago, at a lecture I was attending in Los Angeles, a Buddhist master shared the following humble observation: "Detachment is easy when you're living in the mountains, when there's nothing tempting you or pressuring you. It's hard to be detached when you're living in the city and are surrounded by all the hustle and bustle." Since most of us don't have the luxury of living in the mountains, the only way we can learn detachment is through practice—and your practice begins with the following exercise.

> "For all things and non-things that you may ever want, Friend, understand that sometimes the fastest way to get them is to forget them, and to focus instead on just being the most amazing human being you can be. At which point all of your heart's desires, spoken or unspoken, will be drawn to you more powerfully than a magnet is drawn to steel."
> — *MIKE DOOLEY*

EXERCISE

Next time you come up with a goal in a specific area of your life, carefully visualize what it would look and feel like in your life to have that goal fulfilled, to have it in existence NOW—and then let it go.

Keep doing this until there is no more emotional attachment and only commitment to the perfect outcome. In the process you might find the attachment coming back again and again. Don't worry because that's perfectly normal: just keeping letting go. And when it comes back again, just let go again. It's a process. You know when you're ready when there is a sense of been there, and done that. Yet the commitment remains.

OPTIONAL EXERCISE

There's a particular practice I've found very effective in achieving a state of detachment, though it might not work for all people.

In stressful situations, I visualize a line running through the center of my head right between the centers of my ears. Then I imagine the exact spot on the line that's right in the middle between my ears. Now I focus on this center point until I get closer and closer and I feel that that point is where I am—like it's the focal point of my entire being.

When I'm there solidly, it literally feels as if I'm sitting inside my head, piloting a robot, looking out from inside this robot that is my body, and with two windows that are my eyes, and there's a marvelous sense of clarity and aloofness. I'm engaged and I'm in control, but there's none of the usual turbulence of emotion, reaction, or judgment. What is present is absolute detachment. It is something that the Buddha took a long time to achieve and which you can access in seconds. It works also well when stressed.

Now you can take this on as an exercise and then walk around and see what happens and how it feels. It might surprise you and you might feel a little uncomfortable at first because it is a place completely void of emotion. It may even feel a little scary as we're very much accustomed to feeling a constant stream of emotions.

Now if you don't find your center point automatically when you try this, just keep "adjusting" and probing in the surrounding area until you find where the spot is for you. Just keep trying until you get it—but remember not to get attached!

QUESTIONS

1. In what areas of your life do you find yourself constantly frustrated or upset?

2. Select one area and examine the real source of the dismay or frustration. To what are you so attached?

3. What's been the impact of being so attached in this area of your life?

4. What small, daily practice can you take on to begin cultivating detachment in this area of your life? For instance, it could be as simple as taking five deep breaths whenever you find yourself getting upset and mindfully letting go of the attachment at that moment.

5. What would it provide for you to have detachment in this particular area of your life?

10. THE POWER OF EMPATHY
THE ABILITY TO FEEL SOMEONE'S FEELINGS

ARTWORK BY RENE TRINIDAD ALDONZA

Likely the most important ability in life, business, leadership, marketing, sales, politics, and creativity is the ability to place yourself in someone else's shoes.

Empathy is the ability to place yourself in someone's position and the ability to feel what they feel and understand the background of their thoughts as it relates to them. When this is achieved we have placed ourselves in a state of being called empathy.

Empathy creates a deep understanding for a fellow man or woman, your colleague, business partners, your customers, and even an opponent in warfare. Every husband wishes to understand his wife, every salesperson wishes to understand her clients, every general wishes to understand his enemy, and every player on a sports team wishes to understand the opponent. Empathy is when we can experience reality as they experience reality. It is what some refer to as the ability to place yourself in someone's shoes. When I can see someone else's reality from their perspective, I can gain a much, much deeper understanding of what it is they are going through, their experience of life, what it is they are feeling, what they might be thinking, and the reasoning going through their minds. I say "might" as there are different levels of empathy and the greater the level of empathy the more accurately you will experience the person's reality for yourself. Once achieved, the state of empathy will also allow you to see why and how they make decisions, with great accuracy to predict what their next move will be.

THE POWER OF EMPATHY

Personally I see empathy as one of the most important tools of understanding my clients and my world.

The ability to feel someone's feelings, to vibrate on the same level they do, to hear their thoughts as if they were your own, will allow you to feel the vibration like a tuning fork picking up the frequency of an identical tuning fork.

Potential benefits of Empathy:

- Being able to more fully understand another person, client, market, or potential opponent

- Being able to sense another person's needs

- Helping another unload their load by making them feel understood

- Potentially being able to diffuse a situation with this knowledge

- Being able to foresee or more accurately predict the options and potential next steps of another person

- Understanding a foe or opponent and predicting their moves

- Potentially re-position yourself as an ally, mentor, coach, or friend instead of being seen as an opponent

- Transform a relationship

- Being able to understand and read your client

- Being able to read your target market

- Being more creative in developing solutions for others

- Being able to predict the market and create better products for a new or future market.

Let's explain empathy further with the help of a metaphor. While metaphors are never quite perfect, they can be a great way of putting something into perspective. When we see the feelings and thoughts of a person as a package they want to deliver, then we can see them as someone wanting to deliver that package. And we can also see them suffering under the weight of that package all the way up to the point where they feel you have gotten it, the point when you receive the package, meaning you have not just received the message but also fully understood their reality. This creates trust when they want you to understand them or when they don't mind that you understand them. This trust in turn opens the door to all kinds of new possibilities, including new levels of relatedness, sales, market-share, battle field advantages, you name it, and you can see it in the list above.

When I used to be a supervisor at Mercedes-Benz in Beverly Hills, California I had 70 people under me. It wasn't unusual for me to have to deal with some sort of conflict between a couple of colleagues. When this happened, I would usually pull them into my office and have each of them share their side of what happened while the other had to listen openly and not allowed to talk until I said so. Once each had their opportunity

> "When you start to develop your powers of empathy and imagination, the whole world opens up to you."
> — SUSAN SARANDON

to share what happened, I had the first guy share the *intention* of what he did, followed by the second guy. Again neither was allowed to speak while the other was talking. This usually created enough empathy for both parties such that you could actually see and perceive from their faces that they understood, that it was just a big misunderstanding and that they actually quite liked each other. Empathy in most cases had been established in a very short time. But just to finish it off for good we discussed how we could have handled it better so that next time it won't escalate to that point. Simple really, but it takes a commitment to do it right, plus an assumption that we are all good people at our core.

In an Italian case study published in the September 2012 issue of *Academic Medicine* served "as a follow up to a smaller study published in the same journal in March 2011 from Thomas Jefferson University investigating physician empathy and its impact on patient outcomes. That study included 891 diabetic patients and 29 physicians and concluded similar findings: patients of physicians with high empathy scores had better clinical outcomes than patients of other physicians with lower scores."

In the end, when you don't understand someone, they won't easily allow themselves to be influenced by you if at all, or only with great resistance. You may still be able to persuade them to buy your product or idea, but likely it will be at a much reduced price and much less convincingly so. With empathy it will likely require a lot less arm wrestling if not a more immediate buy-in.

It is easiest to have empathy with someone who is being authentic with us, hence the importance of *authenticity* as explained in another chapter, and of course also trust. Without *trust* there is no authenticity. You can see how each beingness discussed in separate chapters empowers another and how they support each another, thus making their impact exponential.

EXERCISE

> "If you want to take someone to a new place, it is best to meet them where they are and then go there together."
> — *BJORN MARTINOFF*

The simplest way to create empathy with another person is to simply feel yourself what they feel. They will be able to tell what you are feeling by the sound of your voice and the expression of your face as well as your body language followed by a short statement of understanding such as: *"I understand."* Or *"I can get your reality."* Or *"I know how you feel."*

To experience empathy with another person in more difficult cases, physically put yourself into their exact body language and situation. Make sure your entire body matches all of theirs. This includes the angle of their heads, every slightest millimeter of movement in their face, how they sit or stand, where they are looking, how they are breathing, how they position their shoulders. Give yourself permission to feel the feelings that come up no matter what they may be. You may also experience thoughts coming up as well as pictures of places and surroundings. In the beginning you may have to do this with your own body, while when you get better at this you might be able to do and experience this in your mind. Initially, it can take a bit or quite a few physical adjustments before you get it right the first few times but don't let that discourage you. The more accurately you match their physiology the more accurately you will be with reading them and feeling what they feel. Advanced practitioners may even pick up some of their mental images at that moment, no matter how distant in the past.

Welcome to the world of empathy. Empathy is a powerful tool in a world that has little certainty except for the certainty you create yourself.

QUESTIONS

1. In what relationships in your life do you feel as if you're constantly misunderstood?

2. Selecting one of these relationships, recall your last interaction with the person involved with as much detail as possible. Then setting your thoughts and feelings about the person and the relationship aside, ask yourself: What was it like for the other person in that interaction?

3. Going more deeply into the inquiry, ask yourself the following additional questions: What thoughts and feelings probably arose for the other person? Did having those thoughts and feelings make their behavior during that encounter more understandable?

4. Continuing to stay in the other person's shoes, ask yourself: What could you have said or done differently?

5. WhatHow do you think your next interaction with this person would be like if you acted or spoke differently based on empathy?

"If you want to take someone to a new place, it is best to meet them where they are and then go there together."

— BJORN MARTINHOFF

11. THE POWER OF FAITH
CERTAINTY BEYOND LOGIC

Faith is certainty beyond logic and the ability to trust that a desired outcome, or at least an outcome that has your best interests at heart, will be the result of your efforts. It means being able to continue to work toward your goal, without doubting or stopping yourself or your initiative, when the result you're seeking hasn't yet materialized when expected or how you expected it. It also means focusing on what's missing in your efforts rather than giving up all effort entirely.

Just based on everything I've said so far in this chapter as well in the chapter on Detachment, you already get a sense that having faith can be a challenging thing—especially in the times we live in when there's so much pressure to produce immediate results and when there are so many things we could do "instead." We're often told to "do what's practical," or to "cut our losses" or to focus our energies on what's going to get "faster results." There's little room for just allowing time for our efforts to bear their inevitable fruit. I learned how to have faith from a trying experience in my own life. Years ago, I helped turn around a small automotive company in Los Angeles. We were able to turn around this small company and bring it from losing a quarter of a million dollars per month to being profitable, while at the same time having high customer satisfaction ratings.

In that moment, just when I thought I'd be rewarded for my efforts and put on a corporate pedestal, the company was sold and I promptly ended up losing my job. It was at this point, when things were at their lowest for me, that I took one of the biggest leaps of faith in my life: I got rid of my two

ARTWORK BY RENE TRINIDAD ALDONZA

THE POWER OF FAITH

Mercedes Benzes, sold a lot of things on eBay, put the rest of it in storage—and flew to Asia.

Given that I'd just lost my job when I'd actually accomplished something great, starting over again in a place that was completely unknown to me was practically insane.

But the day after I arrived in Asia, a door opened to the career I really wanted: a career in coaching, developing and training people.

Today, I'm settled in Asia, with a thriving and fulfilling executive and organization development company, a lovely wife and four beautiful children. And what made it all possible was sheer faith.

 *Faith consists in believing when it is beyond the power of reason to believe."*
— *VOLTAIRE*

Now if you're thinking that faith is something that's only for the religious, I can reassure you that it's not. Faith transcends religion in the sense that non-believers often exercise some form of faith in their lives.

In fact, if you look into your own life as a creative professional, you'll find that some of your biggest accomplishments often came from your wildest leaps of faith. A lot of this has to do with the nature of the creative endeavor: unless you've begun following a formula in doing what you need to do, there's always an element of unpredictability in how closely your creation matches your intention. In addition, just choosing to be a creative professional is a leap of faith in its own right: there's a tremendous amount of competition these days, and the pace and volume of the work can vary considerable from one month to the next.

So when you take a leap, hold on to faith.

EXERCISE

Find an area in your life where maybe you've nearly given up on something because it seemed as if all your efforts were going nowhere. Find just one area—preferably one that really matters to you, like a hobby or a passion—and commit to taking consistent action in that area even if you don't think you're getting any results. Give yourself a time frame that's appropriate to the area. My only advice is: make sure your timeframe is longer than what you're comfortable with.

Because chances are, you simply haven't given enough faith and time in the past for results to be produced from your actions. In a lot of cases, faith is about being able to wait out that seemingly unproductive time and using it to learn whatever lessons need to be learned.
Try it—I promise that you'll be surprised and delighted by what happens.

QUESTIONS

1. What are some aspirations or dreams you've had in your life that you've given up on because of a perceived lack of progress or success?

2. Picking just one of these aspirations or dreams, ask yourself: Did you really fail? Or did the results simply take more time than you expected to materialize or come in a form that you didn't want or expect?

3. What did it cost you to give up on that particular aspiration or dream?

4. What would it provide for you to take on that aspiration or dream again?

5. What actions would you take if you had the faith-based conviction that your efforts in this area WILL eventually bear fruit?

12. THE POWER OF FLEXIBILITY
THE ABILITY TO ACCOMMODATE ALTERNATIVES

ARTWORK BY RENE TRINIDAD ALDONZA

Once upon a long, long time a neighborhood was beginning to flood.

In one house there was a man all by himself.

A bus comes and the driver asks him to get on the bus to leave the area. But the man says: "No, God is going to save me.'

Than the water rises to a height of several feet forcing the man onto the roof.

A boat comes by to pick him up. But the man says: "No, God is going to save me.'

The waters keep rising.

The man now sits on top of the chimney.

A helicopter comes by. But the man says: "No, God is going to save me.'

The water keeps on rising and the man drowns.

Now he's in front of God and he asks God what happened. He says: "God, I thought you were going to save me!?!"

To which God replies:" Who do you think sent you the bus, and the boat, and the helicopter?"

While I don't know the source of this story, and I don't know whether it is true, it always makes me smile.

People usually think of flexibility as a notion that's opposed to focus. Focus tends to be associated with single-minded determination—like how a horse with blinders behaves—while flexibility tends to be associated with a kind of laidback

THE POWER OF FLEXIBILITY

looseness. Both are generally acknowledged to be positive traits, but are considered paradoxical when put together.

However, flexibility has an important role to play, especially when we already have the focus provided by having a goal or an objective. This is because not all the paths to our goals or objectives will take the form of straight lines (in fact, most of the paths that ultimately lead us to where we want to go never take the form of straight lines!).

Focus (which I treat in a different chapter) refers to our ability to keep our final destination in mind regardless of the circumstances. It's our ability to keep our mind on our goal in the face of the many distractions and temptations life throws our way.

Flexibility, on the other hand, refers to our ability to accommodate alternative and unanticipated ways of achieving our goals.

For instance, if you've decided that your dream vacation is a week in Bali, focus is sticking to "going to Bali" even if your travel agent keeps telling you that there's a promotion going on for a week-long vacation in Phuket. Flexibility, on the other hand, is being willing to try traveling by bus and ferry instead of by plane so you can actually afford that week-long Bali breather.

That's why it actually pays to occasionally explore things that might be a bit "off" sometimes. I'm not telling you to scatter your energies all of the sudden in a hundred different directions. I'm just saying that every so often, it will do you some good to be willing to consider off-beaten tracks to your ultimate destination. So the $50,000 contract someone's offering you isn't the $1,000,000 contract you're looking for—but who knows? Maybe that much smaller contract will be the stepping stone to a series of contracts that will lead you to your $1,000,000 target.

The point is we can only see so far ahead. Opportunities often come up in the guise of seemingly trivial things, like invitations to parties or offers of blind dates. Synchronicity is something that we usually just see on hindsight: people look back and they suddenly perceive a trail of meaningful events that, at the time they happened, seemed completely disconnected and insignificant.

> *Insanity: Doing the same thing over and over again and expecting different results."*
> — ALBERT EINSTEIN

In my own experience, being flexible led to one of the biggest breakthroughs of my life. In the chapter on faith, I talked about how I eventually came to Asia from the United States. Let me say a little bit more about that move here, this time in relation to flexibility.

See, before I made my big move to Asia, I'd already determined what my purpose in life is, which is "to be a trusted advisor to world leaders." At the time I created this statement, Asia was definitely not on the list of places I had for fulfilling this purpose. So when I was considering going to Asia, it was a major concern to me that it seemed to have no connection at all with the purpose I'd set for myself. At the same time, something about Asia excited me. It also frightened me, to be honest, but the excitement was definitely there and it was stronger than the anxiety.

So even though I wasn't sure where it would lead to in terms of my purpose, I went for it. And sure enough, on my second day in the Philippines, I met a man whom I eventually ended up working with—and that engagement eventually led to a professional career in training and development that allowed me to get closer and closer to fulfilling my life purpose!

Here's the other thing that being flexible provided for me: when I first created my purpose of being "a trusted advisor to world leaders," what I had initially meant by that was political world leaders. The leaders I eventually ended up working with were corporate world leaders. If I'd been stuck on just working with political world leaders, I'd have ended up being dissatisfied and unfulfilled. But being flexible about the kinds of leaders I work with has allowed me to flourish in my career. I wouldn't say no to working with political world leaders—I am still very much inspired by that—AND, I'm very happy to be working with corporate world leaders. (That's yet another benefit of being flexible, by the way. You give God (or the universe) the chance to give you something that might lead you to even greater happiness! And not only that, it may eventually lead you to something even more fulfilling.)

So in your life as a creative professional, be alert to these seemingly random opportunities. You might think that this doesn't apply to you because creative work requires a certain amount of flexibility, but I invite you to consider that there are areas in your life where you do happen to be inflexible. When a random opportunity comes up for you in these other areas of life, ask yourself: What's being presented to me at this moment? Because the path to your goal may not look like anything you'll ever expect! And likely it will still lead you in the direction you've been wanting to go.

EXERCISE

> "In the future, instead of striving to be right at a high cost, it will be more appropriate to be flexible and plural at a lower cost. If you cannot accurately predict the future then you must flexibly be prepared to deal with various possible futures."
> — EDWARD DE BONO

Go back into your life and start to pay attention now to the different opportunities that come your way and see how they might be alternative ways of reaching a goal you have in mind. For instance, you might have always wanted to develop or strengthen your leadership skills, and you've been waiting for your job promotion as a chance to do precisely that. Then a friend invites you to take a martial arts course, and you instantly dismiss it because "it's not your thing."

But if you ask me, for instance, I've learned some crucial things about leadership just from watching Bruce Lee—lessons that I now teach to my executive coaching clients and which they hugely appreciate. But that connection between leadership and martial arts won't necessarily be so obvious—and that's exactly why flexibility is necessary.

So when opportunity shows up, trust, be flexible, have faith, and go for it!

THE POWER OF FLEXIBILITY

QUESTIONS

1. In what areas of your life do you have very strict or rigid ideas about how things should be done or how goals should be achieved?

2. Selecting just one of these areas, what's your experience of life in this area?

3. What are some ways you can begin cultivating flexibility in this area? List down at least three ways.

4. What opens up for you as you begin speculating on alternative ways of doing things in this area of your life?

5. What would open up for you if you asked the same questions, but this time applying them in the context of strict or rigid ideas you have about an important person in your life?

13. THE POWER OF FOCUS

THE ABILITY TO KEEP OUR FINAL DESTINATION IN MIND

In the everyday understanding of the word, focus refers to the point on which we train our attention and concentration. Most people are already aware of the importance of focus, but what most people don't know is that there's such a thing as primary focus and secondary focus.

Primary focus and secondary focus are concepts I learned from a race car driving instructor back in the days when I worked for Mercedes-Benz in California. According to him, it's crucial in race car driving to look ahead to the farthest point of the track that you can still see. This farthest point of vision is what is known as primary focus, and the intention behind training your attention on it is to avoid surprises such as rocks on the road, potholes or other surprises that can get really nasty if you see them too late.

I learned this the hard way when I was about 24 years old. On a dark night, I was exiting a small village on a German highway. I was driving with a couple of friends in my freshly restored 1967 Buick Skylark convertible. With the Buick's 5.7 liter V8 engine, it occurred to me that I could easily overtake the five cars ahead of me all at once. Not having any idea of what the primary focus was at the time, all my attention was on the first car I was attempting to overtake. Just when I was driving past it, the third car up ahead pulled out of its lane and got onto my lane to overtake the car ahead of it—and I was right behind this car at 200 kilometers per hour and accelerating.

Through an unimaginable stroke of luck, I was able to avoid the car. I hit my brakes HARD and my car swung around with the rear brakes locking up and I ended up on the other side of a ditch. I didn't hit the other car and nobody got hurt but there was a LOT of damage to my Buick. The front end, the grill and the hood were badly warped.

Now, if I had kept all the cars ahead in my field of vision by focusing on the furthest car ahead, and not just on the one that I was trying to overtake, I likely would have been able to make the necessary corrections quicker and sooner and avoid the entire mess in which I had suddenly found myself.

And this is a mistake novice car drivers tend to make. Most new car drivers will only focus as far as fifty to one hundred meters ahead. Such a limited field of vision prevents us from seeing obstacles further up ahead such as rocks, potholes and even a small child running across the street. By the time we notice them, we'll only have a few seconds left to react—not enough time in a lot of cases to choose the appropriate response, much less the desired outcome or result.

If it happens in driving, it also happens in decision-making. Often, we make the wrong decisions because so little time is available to thoroughly consider them. These wrong decisions then delay us from achieving our goal by either getting us off track, or worse, derailing us altogether.

So in life, just like on the road or on the race track, it's important not just to focus on the immediate objective you have in mind—the secondary focus—but on the ultimate objective that lies far ahead in the horizon—the primary focus. Secondary focus means looking ahead to where you immediately need to go while primary focus means looking as far ahead as possible.

This is especially critical in long-term creative endeavors of any kind, whether it's writing a novel, directing a film or mounting an exhibit. You need secondary focus to get all the little details and intermediate steps handled, but you also need primary focus to stay in touch with the reason why all the little details and intermediate steps are even important! Without secondary focus, you can't do what needs to be done daily with diligence and precision. But without primary focus, you lose your connection with the inspiration and vision that are needed to sustain your daily work.

The beauty of maintaining your primary focus is that your far-off objective always remains in your line of sight—even when you're looking at and dealing with what's immediately ahead.

> "One reason so few of us achieve what we truly want is that we never direct our focus; we never concentrate our power. Most people dabble their way through life, never deciding to master anything in particular."
> — TONY ROBBINS

EXERCISE

Take a long-term goal you have in one area of your life and break it down into intermediate objectives or milestones. Milestones are smaller-scale achievements that function as stepping stones to your ultimate goal.

For example, if your long-term goal is to run a marathon, good milestones would be quitting smoking, buying running shoes and finishing a ten kilometer run. Milestones are good ways of assessing whether you're on track to achieving your goal or not. In the context of focus, your end goal is your primary focus and your milestones are your secondary focus.

So while it's good to devote your attention to getting your lungs in shape and in getting the right kinds of footgear, every so often it's worthwhile to just "look up" and out into the horizon and to remember what it's all for—which is to run or even win a marathon.

Focusing way ahead will keep your decision making in alignment with that primary goal. It will help guide you to make the right choices and decisions along the way. But if you only focus on the next step, the choice you'll make may be appropriate for that next step but may not necessarily be the appropriate choice for your long-term or primary goal.

Note: In a creative project, it's very useful to start team meetings by revisiting the project's vision and any long-term goals briefly just to get everyone into the right frame of mind.

QUESTIONS

1. In what areas of your life do you experience feeling ineffective or thwarted?

2. Selecting just one of these areas, can you identify what your primary focus is?

3. Can you then identify what your secondary focus is? (There can be quite a few of them.)

4. Is your feeling of ineffectiveness or frustration possibly coming from not adequately working on both your primary and secondary focus points?

5. What actions can you take in this area to address both the primary and secondary focus points? List down at least five.

"Concentrate all your thoughts upon the work at hand. The sun's rays do not burn until brought to a focus."

— ALEXANDER GRAHAM BELL

14. THE POWER OF FUN

REFRAME WHAT YOU'RE DOING INTO A GAME

The subject of power can be invested with so much significance that it's rarely, if ever, associated with having fun. But if we stop to consider it, we're most compelling when we're having fun, most productive when we're having fun and most effective when we're having fun. Hence power is a by-product of having fun and I've seen this demonstrated by what my friend, Jim, has achieved.

Jim used to run a car dealer—one of the best in California and in the world. He transformed it from a tiny dealer in an out-of-the-way suburb into one of the biggest dealers in Los Angeles in just a few short years. At the time that I met him, he had just succeeded in growing his business 20 percent the previous year in a market that had actually shrunk by 20 percent. How Jim did it was by having fun—by transforming what his people would otherwise think of as mere work into challenging and enjoyable games. On the floor, I've seen him invent spontaneous games, once yelling at the top of his lungs that "the one who sells the next car gets an extra $2,000!" He would do this sort of thing regularly, though with lots of variations. I do hope he'll write a book about his experiences in the near future.

Jim actively applies what many of us have always instinctively known: that having fun is important and that relating to what we do as a game is empowering.

We not only perform better when we're having fun and when things are going well, but the fun also offsets the less pleasurable emotions that inevitably come up in anything that we do—especially during periods of crisis or setback. Fun makes it easier for us to persist even

ARTWORK BY RENE TRINIDAD ALDONZA

when we're not succeeding because we are genuinely enjoying the process rather than being merely attached to its outcome. And one of the best ways for us to have fun is to re-contextualize or reframe what we're doing into a game. This applies just as much in the creative field as it does in any other profession! Although many people think that being a creative professional is often fun and games (an image bolstered by what's typically portrayed in the media), the pressure of having to meet tight deadlines and even tighter budgets WHILE still being expected to come up with something original can be the exact opposite of fun, to say the least. In these instances, and especially in these instances, it pays to step back for a moment and to think: how can I put some fun back into this?

In short, if you want to have power in a particular situation, see if you can turn what you're up to into some kind of game, where playing the game, and eventually winning can be fun for you and those playing the game with you. (Just be responsible and make sure that what's fun for you doesn't harm someone else!)

> "People rarely succeed unless they have fun in what they are doing."
> — *DALE CARNEGIE*

82 THE POWER OF FUN

■ EXERCISE

Look at your goals and see what kind of games you can create around them that will make them fun for you to win. For example, one game I frequently play is the game of treating-myself-to-a-full-body-massage-if-I-win-a-client-tomorrow or a dinner with my wife at my favorite place for finishing a proposal on time. Of course, it's easier to create fun games in some situations than it is in others, such as paying off a debt or making an apology. But the more challenging the circumstances are, the greater are the likely rewards.

One last thought: include your family, your friends, your colleagues—and, when possible, even your clients—in the games that you play.

Fun is infectious, and the more people have it, the more it will empower you and those around you to succeed!

QUESTIONS

1. In what areas of your life do you feel as if the fun's just completely disappeared?

2. Selecting one of these areas, what's life like for you in that area of your life?

3. What things can you do that would start injecting fun back into this area of your life?

4. What would it provide for you to have fun again in this area of your life?

5. What would it provide for the people around you if you were to have fun again in this area of your life?

15. THE POWER OF GRATITUDE

CHOOSING TO BE GRATEFUL

One of the simplest and most effective yet also most overlooked ways of generating power lies in choosing to be grateful.

In the chapter on INTERPRETATION, I talk about how power can be generated by choosing particular ways of interpreting life or viewing life. Gratitude is one of those ways of looking at life that's enormously empowering.

Why? Because in choosing to be grateful, you start focusing on all the things about yourself and your life that deserve to be appreciated. This in itself is already an enormous benefit given that we almost never think about what works in our life.

(We're usually too fixated on all the things that don't work in our lives, e.g., having clients that don't understand anything about the creative endeavor, being bothered by interruptions all the time, running out of inspiration just when you need it, finding out that the new "idea" you just conceived the other day has actually been executed by someone else, and so on and so forth.)

What gratitude achieves are the following things:

- We correct the usually distorted view we have of ourselves and our lives by being present to what's good rather than just the bad.

- We realize that life isn't so bad after all, or that things aren't even bad at all.

- We start to realize that even the things we think are bad have some purpose to serve or some lesson to teach

- We start to realize that we possess far more resources or capabilities than we ever thought we possessed.

By simply introducing a more balanced perspective or by getting us present to the blessings in our life, gratitude gives us enormous power.

But gratitude also serves a very practical purpose—which is to preserve and even increase the presence of those things for which we're

ARTWORK BY RENE TRINIDAD ALDONZA

> "As we express our gratitude, we must never forget that the highest appreciation is not to utter words, but to live by them."
> — *JOHN F. KENNEDY*

grateful.

How?

Well, if you believe in the Law of Attraction, which is simply a statement of the principle that like attracts like, then gratitude simply attracts more gratitude. Said another way, the Law of Attraction states that we tend to bring about that which is the constant focus of our attention. Since gratitude has us focus our attention on the things we like having in our life, we end up having even more of these things in our life.

Conversely, when we're not practicing gratitude, we're usually griping about the things we don't like having in our life. Following the Law of Attraction, by keeping our attention on the things we don't like, we end up having even more of the things that we don't like.

Even if you don't believe in the Law of Attraction, the argument that gratitude helps preserve and even increase the presence of the things for which we're grateful still holds.

Why?

Because when we appreciate something, we exert more effort to take care of it and to not squander it. Things we're not grateful for tend to disappear or deteriorate because of neglect.

When you start feeling grateful for your health, for instance, you'll find yourself doing more things to stay healthy, like eating less and exercising more. Or when you start feeling grateful for your children, you'll find yourself spending more time at home and less time in the office. And by taking better care of your health or spending more time with your children, you'll end up with more things in these areas for which to be grateful. How I personally practice being grateful is that every morning, I light a candle on my altar and thank God for every single thing in my life for which I'm grateful. I give thanks for my business, my clients, my wife and my children—especially my children. I do this every morning and it sets an amazing tone for the rest of my day.

Now here's the bonus about gratitude: it's really easy to apply and a lot of its benefits are instantaneous. Some of the exercises in this workbook aren't necessarily fun to do because they ask you to confront certain things, but taking on being grateful is one of those fun exercises that also provide instant gratification. Just try the next exercise and see for yourself.

> "Gratitude makes sense of our past, brings peace for today, and creates a vision for tomorrow."
> — *MELODY BEATTIE*

THE POWER OF GRATITUDE

EXERCISE

Look into your life and identify the areas where you're unhappy, upset, discontent and/or resigned. The area can be your career, your family, your health, your spirituality or even all of the above.

Write down all of these areas, and then one by one, start listing all the things in these areas for which you can be grateful. It can be a small thing (e.g., not having a car means I get to walk and exercise; not having a job yet means I get to spend more time with the children; etc.). It can even be something that hasn't even happened yet (e.g., I'll be a much stronger person after this setback; I'll finally learn how to be independent after this breakup is over; etc.).

The point is: Don't hold back. Use your creativity and even have fun! I promise you that doing this exercise will have an immediate impact on your level of power. And if you take on doing it on a regular basis, then you'll be expanding your power even more.

QUESTIONS

1. In what areas of your life do you find a sense of gratitude completely missing?

2. Selecting one of these areas, what's your experience of life like in this area?

3. What thoughts come to mind for you the moment you think of this area of your life?

4. Can you begin to see the connection between the thoughts you automatically have about this area of your life and your experience of life in this area?

5. What are the things you can be grateful for in this area of your life? List down at least five and see how your view and experience of this area of your life begin to shift.

16. THE POWER OF GROWTH
DEVELOPING NEW THOUGHT HABITS AND ACTION PATTERNS

ARTWORK BY RENE TRINIDAD ALDONZA

I asked once my friend Angie what she thought of whenever she heard the word "growth." Her answer to me was: "Pain." "Pain?" I asked. "What is it about growth that you find painful?"

She said: "Having to change everything all over again."

Angie's honest response expresses something that we all feel in different degrees about growth—that growth is uncomfortable because it involves change.

But why do we even dislike change to begin with?

Very simply: human beings dislike change because change disrupts our sense of certainty, predictability and control—the three things that contribute to making us feel safe. Knowing how things are allows us to anticipate how things will be—and by anticipating events, we can better influence and control them.

For instance, knowing that a paycheck is going to come in regular two week intervals allows us to plan and time our expenses in a particular way. But when the timing and frequency of that paycheck is suddenly changed, say to once every quarter instead, that alteration means having to adjust everything that's related to how we spend our money. That adjustment is often a difficult thing, because it involves developing new habits of thought and new patterns for action.

I had a personal experience of this early in my career. For a few years, I worked with a part-time consultancy that was completely unpredictable when it came to paying their partners. Sometimes it took three days for me to get paid; sometimes it took a year. It was a very disconcerting time for me because I couldn't plan my financial future working with a company like that. I had no idea what was coming or when it was coming. In the end, I removed myself from that partnership even if it was a significant source of income because the

THE POWER OF GROWTH

money simply wasn't worth all the stress coming from the uncertainty.

This is why human beings find growth painful. Growth is painful because growth always involves change—change that unsettles our sense of certainty, predictability and control. We're conditioned to believe that growth is a good thing, yet we find ourselves resisting it at times (maybe even a lot of times). Why we resist it is because we know it will involve change, and change means we need to do the work needed to adapt.

But what people need to realize is that even if growth and change are painful (or at least inconvenient), growth and change are also indicators of our vitality and power.

For instance, if you look at plants, a plant that isn't growing is literally a plant that's already dying. The same thing applies to human beings: as much as we need certainty and stability, we also need change and variety. My friend Anthony Robbins hit the nail on the head when he said that two of the six fundamental human needs are certainty and variety. The two might seem to contradict each other, but the fact is, being human often involves balancing paradoxical things. So to go back to growth: when we don't grow—or when we refuse to grow—a little piece of us dies. We might get more and more comfortable keeping things exactly the way they are, but we'll discover over time that the comfort and the convenience don't really make us happy. In fact, they might lead to us getting downright depressed. And that's simply because as human beings we're designed to grow—and when we're growing and expanding, we're actually very powerful. Consider how this principle might apply to your life as a creative professional. In what ways can you grow in your field? To return to our analogy of the plant, is your growth opportunity branching out horizontally, that is, expanding your skills to fields related to your line of work? Or is your growth opportunity rooting down vertically, that is, deepening your mastery of your particular skill? Have you "wilted" without noticing it and foregone growth altogether? If yes, notice how this has impacted your work as a creative professional and use the following exercise to jumpstart growing again!

> "All the evidence that we have indicates that it is reasonable to assume in practically every human being, and certainly in almost every newborn baby, that there is . . . an impulse towards growth, or towards the actualization."
> —ABRAHAM MASLOW

....
....
....
....
....
....

EXPONENTIAL POWER FOR CREATIVE DESIGN PROFESSIONALS HANDBOOK

THE POWER OF GROWTH

■ EXERCISE

> " *Intellectual growth should commence at birth and cease only at death*
> — ALBERT EINSTEIN

Take a class. Do a course. Read a book. Learn a language. Meet someone new. Whatever it is, grow and develop yourself in at least one area. It might be uncomfortable and it might be inconvenient, but I promise you that it will expand your power.

QUESTIONS

1. In what areas of your life do you feel as if you're stagnating or just maintaining the status quo?

2. Selecting just one of these areas, what's it like for you inhabiting this space of stagnation or status quo preservation?

3. Working with the same area, what small, practical and easily achievable things can you take on to introduce some "growth" in this area? List down at least five things.

4. What would it provide for you to experience some revitalizing growth in this area of your life?

5. What small, practical and easily achievable things can you do in daily life to increase your experience of growth in general?

17. THE POWER OF HUMILITY
OPENS DOORS, HEARTS AND MINDS

ARTWORK BY RENE TRINIDAD ALDONZA

Humility is something you might not expect in a list of chapters in a workbook about power. How, you may ask, is humility related to all the other chapters?

Let me step back for a moment and ask you: Whom do you see as the most powerful people in history? I mean those who had a positive impact; not those who had a negative impact.

The kind of people that come to my mind are Jesus Christ, Mahatma Gandhi, Martin Luther King, Nelson Mandela, Mother Teresa and the Dalai Lama. All of them were unquestionably powerful people, having influenced millions of lives, whole nations and entire generations.

What made these people so successful? What made them so impactful? Why did people listen to them? Why are they still remembered even today? Yes, they were exceptional as they all achieved amazing results, and yes, they did extraordinary things that nobody had done before, and yes, they were some of the most influential people on earth. Yet they all had one quality that distinguished them from other powerful people and that quality was HUMILITY.

The most powerful people in history were not just powerful—they were powerful and humble. Now how can this be? Don't power and humility contradict each other?

The answer is no. They actually support each other. Like the principles of yin and yang, they balance each other out and make the other more effective. Humility without power won't get you anywhere. And power without humility will simply become FORCE. And we all know that tend to push back and resist people when they're pushed or forced. It's humility that opens doors, opens hearts and opens minds. It gives people a choice to buy in and the option to align while force will wrestle—maybe even sell—but rarely inspire. One thing I've noticed from watching the World Cup for years is that the team that does well in the early rounds tends to get too sure of itself and ends up not taking its next game as seriously as the team that barely survives the first round. And sure enough, this complacency leads the team to lose its subsequent games and the chance to become the World Champion.

In the creative life, humility can take the form of relinquishing past accomplishments and successes and returning to what the late Zen master Shunryu Suzuki called the "beginner's mind." By continuously surrendering the notion that you're an "expert" in what you do—whether it's writing, illustrating or taking photographs—you maintain an attitude of openness, receptivity and wonder that's critical to fostering ongoing creativity.

Hence, there is a real lesson to be found in humility. When we're too sure of ourselves, we tend to take things too easily and make mistakes, or, we pass up opportunities to learn new things and get better at what we do.

> "The most positively impactful and memorable leaders in history have always been both powerful and humble."
> — *BJORN MARTINOFF*

EXERCISE

When I notice that I'm becoming too sure of myself, I remind myself to remain humble. There have been occasions in my life and in my career when I thought that I knew it all, and guess what happened next? Life proved to me that I didn't! And it tends to be a pretty humiliating experience when it happens.

Now I just remind myself to remain humble in the first place. Will it be a piece of cake always? Not really. It's a practice to take on.

And the more I practice, the better I become.

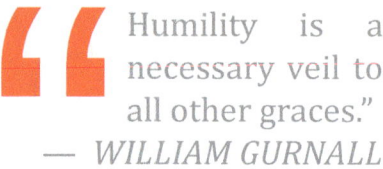

" Humility is a necessary veil to all other graces."
— *WILLIAM GURNALL*

QUESTIONS

1. In what areas of your life is it easy for you to feel arrogant, complacent or on top of things?

2. Picking just one of these areas, imagine what would it be like for you if things fell apart in this area of your life? How would you feel? What would you think? How would you react?

3. Keeping this scenario in mind, how would you feel, think or act differently in this area of your life?

4. What small, practical and easily achievable practices can you take on in this area of your life to cultivate an attitude of humility?

5. What would cultivating an attitude of humility provide for you in this area of your life?

18. THE POWER OF INSPIRATION

WHAT FILLS YOU WITH PASSION AND INCITES YOU TO TAKE ACTION

People usually think of inspiration as something that happens mostly to artists and geniuses. If we happen to feel inspired every so often, that's a great thing. But feeling inspired all of the time or even just most of the time seems like a lot to ask for or expect—even for people who are engaged in creative work!

But I assert that the absence of inspiration from our daily lives is what turns our commitments into shackles. Commitments, duties, obligations and responsibilities which are devoid of any inspiration become lead weights—things that, at the very least, hold us back from what we really want, and at the very worst, actually drag us down. Said another way, they become things that we dread:

Dread. Dread. Dread. Dread.

Dread. Monday...

ARTWORK BY RENE TRINIDAD ALDONZA

Dread. Dread. Dread. Dread.

Dread. Wednesday...

Dread. Dread. Dread. Dread.

Dread. Sunday...

Dread. Dread. Dread. Dread.

Dread. A quarter later...

Dread. Dread. Dread. Dread.

Dread. Five years later...

These things that we dread are what we usually call a "job" or a "relationship"—and for those of us who've done the dreading long enough, we usually call it a "career" or a "marriage." Hence if our jobs or relationships don't last, many times it's because the inspiration has disappeared.

At this point, you might be asking: "But isn't inspiration beyond my control? Sometimes I feel it and sometimes I just don't! It's not like there's something I can actually do about it."

On the contrary, you can generate inspiration. If you look at all the things in your life that have inspired you—that have filled you with passion and incited you to take action—you'll notice that there's probably a pattern to them. The more you can identify what this

THE POWER OF INSPIRATION

pattern is and the clearer you can get about what's common behind all these incidents, the greater will be your ability to generate inspiration for yourself.

Why?

Because the moment you know what inspires you, you can start looking at all your commitments, duties, obligations and responsibilities from the perspective of your inspiration.

For instance, if alleviating poverty inspires you, and you're working (maybe not very happily) as a copy writer in a multinational ad agency, you can pause to consider how what you do actually helps create jobs in the market and thereby alleviates poverty in a very significant way. Just like that, something that was a lead weight in one moment becomes a pair of wings in another moment. Imagine the kind of power you'll have in your work (and in your relationships) when you actually start seeing them as ways to fulfill on what inspires you!

Now, when you start looking for what it is that inspires you, here's a tip:

It's likely something that will challenge you enormously.

I'm not making the above statement as a prescription—like it's something you should do. Rather, I'm saying it as a description—as something, in other words, that I've seen based on a lot of experience. For instance, part of the work I do when I coach executives is to ask them to come up with ideas on how they can grow their business by 8 percent in one quarter. It usually takes a long time for the group to come up with suggestions, and they're usually not voiced with a lot of enthusiasm.

But when I ask the same group to think of how to grow their results by 200 percent, suddenly the entire room lights up! Everyone starts coming up with ideas and I have to struggle to write down everything they're saying fast enough.

So based on my observations, asking people to deliver 8 percent barely gets them going. Ask them to deliver 200 percent instead, and it's as if they've drunk ten cups of coffee!

Why is this so? Logic tells us that it should be easier to develop ideas around an 8 percent goal versus a 200 percent goal. But that's never been the case in my experience. This is why I assert that human beings are wired to find inspiration in going after what challenges them.

You can see this by observing children or even just by remembering how you were as a child. When you were five years old, I don't think you said "I want to grow up and be second best!" or "I want to grow up and settle for something less than what I want!" No, I assert that when you were five years old, you probably said things like: "I want to win the Nobel Prize for Literature when I grow up!" or "I want to do an underwater documentary of the Marianas Trench!" or "I want my paintings to be exhibited all over the world!" In other words, we just aren't built to be inspired by small games. For instance, if you were given the choice, would you rather devote your life to writing a book that could influence the lives of 500 people or one that could influence the lives of 5,000,000 people?

I'm willing to bet on what your answer's likely to be.
For me personally, I've observed that it inspires me a lot more to talk to the top executives of an

organization rather than its middle managers. This isn't because I have something against middle managers, but because my intention is always to make the biggest difference possible with the training programs that I offer. And when I'm talking to the head of a company rather than the head of a department, I'm clear that I have an opportunity to influence the lives of 2,000 people versus, say, 200 people. And that's something that personally inspires me.

"Inspiration is aliveness in relationship to a goal."
— MARIA VICTORIA PEÑAFLOR MARTINOFF

EXERCISE

Take a look into your life and see if there are areas that in which you'd like to see more inspiration. Pick one area that, if transformed, can give you the most juice in life. Ask yourself: How can I re-contextualize, reframe or give some new exciting meaning to this area so that I can't wait to get out of bed in the morning just to focus on it?

Now, don't feel bad and don't give up if you can't come up with an answer right away. If this thing has been dreadful to you for years, it's perfectly understandable if you find the exercise enormously challenging.

If you're in this situation, one way to start is by identifying all the things about this area that somehow contributes to fulfilling the things that inspire you. This might demand a lot of objectivity and generosity on your part, but stick to the exercise. Do it over several stretches if necessary, but don't stop until you begin to sense a glimmer of that inspiration that you haven't felt in a really long time.

Now, just a brief note: People think that only the "lofty" things in life are worthy of inspiration (like truth or justice or peace), which isn't true. It's also crucial to consider how challenging the source of your inspiration is, not because I want you to have a difficult life, but simply because if something doesn't challenge you, it's just not likely to inspire you!

So the true test in assessing a source of inspiration is in how it literally gives you life: you're lit up by it, you're filled with energy, and you can't wait to act. With inspiration, what you normally view as work and drudgery becomes joy and pleasure. This is why inspiration is an enormously empowering thing.

"You have to find something that makes your soul sing, something that's going to pull you forward naturally and effortlessly."
— BJORN MARTINOFF

QUESTIONS

1. What areas of your life are missing a sense of inspiration right now?

2. Picking one of these areas, what's your experience of life in this particular area?

3. What would you be able to accomplish in this area if you found inspiration again?

4. Could you generate inspiration in this area by creating a new challenge? If yes, what would that challenge be?

5. Could you generate inspiration in this area by connecting or reconnecting it to your values? If yes, what would those values be and how does this area of your life help you express those values?

19. THE POWER OF INTEGRITY

DOING WHAT YOU SAID YOU WOULD DO

One of the most powerful tools I've ever encountered in my efforts to develop and train myself is the notion of integrity as defined by Werner Erhard, founder of EST and Landmark Education.

At the simplest level, Werner defines having integrity as simply doing what you said you would do, the way it was meant to be done, by when you said you would do it. And when you realize that you're not going to get something done or done on time, integrity involves telling the people who'll be affected right away—with an intention to address the impact on them.

The benefit of integrity defined this way is mind-bogglingly simple. As Werner puts it, it just makes things work.

One example of how integrity makes things work comes from an experience I had a few years ago when we conducted a workshop in Japan with my former partner Jerry.

After Jerry and I were done with our preparations, we decided to do some sightseeing and visit Odawara Castle. To get to the Castle, we needed to take a shuttle bus from our hotel to the train station down the hill and then take the train the rest of the way to the site.

The first thing I noticed when I looked at the hotel's notice board was that the shuttle's first trip to the train station was scheduled to leave at 10:12 am—not 10:00 am or 10:15am, which I would have expected, but 10:12 am.

And sure enough, when Jerry and I got settled on the shuttle, we noticed a large digital clock on the inside of the shuttle above the door and at exactly 10:11 am and

ARTWORK BY RENE TRINIDAD ALDONZA

59 seconds, the door of the shuttle closed and there was probably nothing that could have stopped it. And we set off for the train station. I had the sense that if I had come running at the moment the doors began to close, the shuttle bus driver would likely NOT have opened the doors for me. Sounds cruel? But wait, there is more to the story...

When we got to the station, we had a hard time figuring out how to operate the ticket

THE POWER OF INTEGRITY

machine. Because of this, we arrived at the platform just a few seconds late—and basically missed the train.

That was how I found things to be in Japan for the rest of my trip: everything was timed to start at a precise moment and there was no waiting or delaying for people who didn't show up at the precise moment.

The logic of this is self-evident. For instance, once there's a delay in the schedule of just one train, it impacts the schedule of countless other trains, causing further and bigger delays along the line. Hence, waiting for just one tardy passenger can hold up hundreds, and potentially even thousands, of other people.

So integrity at this really simple level—the level of just being on time for a shuttle or a train—already goes a tremendous way in making things work. If you look at the countries in the world that are more successful than others, a lot of their success boils down to just having integrity: people stopping at red lights, people throwing their garbage in rubbish bins, people paying their taxes on time (or just paying their taxes, period!).

And integrity is not as complicated or as daunting as it looks. People spend a lot of time and energy justifying why they didn't get things done or why they didn't get them done on time. In my experience, it usually takes far less time and energy just doing the thing as opposed to justifying why it didn't get done.

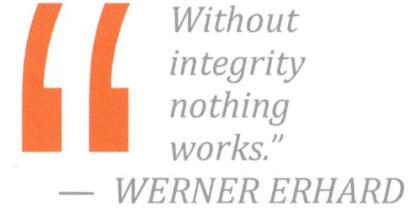

"Without integrity nothing works."
— WERNER ERHARD

For instance, instead of complaining all the time about how getting stuck in traffic makes you late for your meetings with your clients, grab an audio book instead and just leave thirty minutes earlier than usual. You'll be on time, you won't be upset, and you'll even have learned something new!

The same principle applies to that book you want to write, that website you need to complete and those photographs you have to edit. The point is: if you say you're going to do it, just go ahead and do it. Not only will it increase your productivity, it'll boost your confidence and your peace of mind—which will also do wonders for your creativity.

In short, try integrity. It really works.

THE POWER OF INTEGRITY

■ EXERCISE

> "Real integrity is doing the right thing, knowing that nobody's going to know whether you did it or not."
> — OPHRAH WINFREY

Let's work on a simple thing that most people find very difficult. It's the same thing I gave as an example in this chapter, which is being on time.

This is the exercise: be on time—for everything. Be on time for your appointments at home, for your appointments at work and even for appointments with yourself. If you say you'll be up at 5:00 am to go running, but up at 5:00 am to go running. If you tell your wife you're picking her up at 6:00 pm to go on a date, be at her office by 5:55 pm to pick her up for your date. If you tell your son you'll be at his game by 7:00 am, then be at his game by 6:55 am.

I kid you not: the greater the percentage of time that you're on time, or even better, a little early for your appointments, the more people (including yourself) will trust and respect you. It seems like a really small thing, but it goes a really, really long way.

QUESTIONS

1. In what areas of your life are things simply not working?

2. Selecting just one of these areas, ask yourself: Do you consistently do what you'll say you'll do in this area of your life? Ignore the reasons that come up whenever you think of an instance where you don't do what you say you'll do.

3. Can you begin to see the connection between your lack of integrity in this area and the absence of workability?

4. What small, practical and easily achievable things can you take on in this area of your life to begin restoring integrity?

5. What would it provide for you to restore integrity in this area of your life?

20. THE POWER OF INTERPRETATION
AUTOMATIC ANDN ONGOING

ARTWORK BY RENE TRINIDAD ALDONZA

People often think of interpretation as a very deliberate action. What I mean to say by that is that people tend to believe that they only "interpret" things when they're required to do so by particular circumstances, like when they have to make sense of an abstract work of art or figure out what's happening in a confusing situation.

However, what most people don't realize is that the act of interpretation is automatic and ongoing—in other words, we're always interpreting things even if we're not making an effort. It's important for us to really get this because our interpretations have a direct impact on our experience of life.

Let me give an example:

My friend Angie was walking in the mall the other day when a good-looking man rushed by and bumped her hard on the shoulder. Because the impact was quite severe, Angie's first impulse was to yell out: "Watch where you're going, you @#(!&!"

Now if you pay attention to what Angie was tempted to say, it's the logical thing to do if your interpretation of the incident is: "I got hit because there was an imbecile who wasn't paying attention to where he was going."

But like I asked Angie later on, was this the only possible interpretation of this scenario? As Angie grudgingly admitted, there were lots of other ways to look at what had happened, such as:

- He was running after his little boy who wandered away.

- Somebody got hurt and he was rushing off to help.

THE POWER OF INTERPRETATION

- His parking meter was about to expire.

- He got a bad case of the stomach cramps and needed to reach the toilet in time.

- He thought Angie was cute and just wanted to get her attention.

If you consider each of the interpretations above, you'll notice that each one results in a different emotional response. In the interpretation where the man is rushing off to help, for instance, you would probably feel admiration. In the interpretation where he has a bad case of the stomach cramps, you would probably feel sympathy. And in the interpretation where he wants to get Angie's attention, you would probably feel flattered (if you were in Angie's shoes) or amused (if you were in mine).

> "Things don't change. You change your way of looking, that's all."
> — CARLOS CASTAÑEDA

The point is, interpretations play a powerful role in our experience of life, like I said earlier, and we make interpretations like Angie's all of the time—interpretations that anger, annoy, frustrate, irritate, offend or depress us.

The worst part is, our initial interpretations might not even be accurate (they rarely are, to be completely honest). How many of us have experienced disliking a person at first sight because they dressed or talked in a certain way, and then discovering upon further interaction that they were really quite likeable?

We can't prevent many of the things that life throws at us (in the same way that Angie couldn't have prevented that man from running into her), but we do have a say about how events in life affect us by paying attention to the interpretations we make of these events. Since we can't validate which of our possible interpretations is more accurate in a lot of cases anyway, it would be best if we used that "freedom" as the space to choose interpretations that are empowering versus disempowering.

For instance, Angie never got to find out if the man who bumped into her really was just being careless or really just needed to handle an emergency. But guess which interpretation would likelier have left her at peace?

For me, at least, the choice seems pretty obvious.

The bottom-line is: don't allow your interpretations to rob you of your power. Since they're your interpretations anyway, you might as well choose the ones that leave you empowered. In this regard, use the creativity you already possess to come up with the interpretations that leave you with the most power in life!

EXERCISE

Pick something that happened to you in the last week that left you feeling very upset. It can be a major thing like a setback at work or a minor thing like getting held up in traffic. Whatever the event is list down at least ten different interpretations of it.

Now, this can be very difficult at first—especially if you're absolutely convinced that your assessment of things is the right assessment. (Have you noticed that you're always right, by the way?) But if you persist in this exercise and really take it seriously, you'll begin to realize that each interpretation you come up with is really just that: an interpretation.

Of course, some interpretations might be more far-fetched than others, but I'm certain that you'll also come up with interpretations that are as plausible as your initial assessment without being as disempowering.

(As you do this exercise, you might even begin to realize something else: which is that the likelier you are to believe in a given interpretation, the higher your chances are of finding evidence to support it!)

Here's something else I encourage you to try while doing this exercise, which is to pay attention to the emotional response that each interpretation generates.

Every interpretation results in a different emotion: some are positive, some are negative and some are neutral. Allow yourself to fully feel the emotion that comes with each interpretation. At the end of the exercise, ask yourself: "Which of these emotions would I rather feel more often in my life?"

And once you've answered that, ask yourself: "What kinds of interpretation tend to result in these kinds of emotion?"

In answering this question, you'll have discovered for yourself a powerful and effective means of altering your experience of life without having to worry about controlling external events.

THE POWER OF INTERPRETATION

■ QUESTIONS

1. In what areas of your life do you find yourself disempowered?

2. Selecting just one of these areas, what's your interpretation of yourself and your circumstances in this area of your life?

3. Pretend you're playing a game, and the game is to create as many plausible interpretations of yourself and your circumstances in this area of your life. What other interpretations can you come up with? List down at least five.

4. What thoughts and feelings are generated by these different interpretations? List down what comes up for each of the five interpretations.

5. Which of these interpretations do you find the most empowering? Does it make sense to choose this interpretation?

21. THE POWER OF LUCK

THE INTERSECTION BETWEEN OPPORTUNITY AND PREPARATION

When I ask people what they think luck is, what I often hear them say is:

"It' something I wish I had more of."

"It's one of those good things that you can never expect."

"It's a superstition."

In other words, people tend to think of luck as a positive yet uncontrollable and unpredictable occurrence—something that you can pray for or wish for but never really expect.

However, I have a different view of luck, which is that luck is simply the intersection of opportunity and preparation. I'll say that again: luck is what happens when a person creates and prepares for the opportunities they want.

Let me share a personal example. I've been wanting to

ARTWORK BY RENE TRINIDAD ALDONZA

write a book (this workbook that you're holding in your hands is an offshoot of that book) for ten years. But it didn't happen during those ten years simply because I wasn't preparing for it to happen and I wasn't creating opportunities for it to happen. I wasn't creating an outline, or taking down notes, or even telling people that I was interested in writing a book! Then a day came when I finally told myself: Alright Bjorn, you're going to get that book written this year. The next thing I knew, I was at a juice bar chatting with a friend when she casually mentioned being a freelance writer. I immediately said: "Really? Well, I happen to need a writer who can help me write my book!"

Just like that, I got the resource I needed to do something I'd wanted to do for a decade! Some people would call it luck, but it happened simply because I was finally prepared and I was alert to any opportunities coming my way.

And like I mentioned earlier, opportunities can be created—you don't even need to wait for them to happen. For instance, artists who say they want their work to be discovered can act as if someone's just going to notice their talent from out of the blue. But if you want your work to be discovered, you need to create opportunities for your work to be seen (or read, or heard, or viewed,

THE POWER OF LUCK

as the case might be). That could mean setting up a website and a few social media accounts, having copies of your work on your smart phone or tablet for easy access and presentation, and actually talking to people about what you do! Of course, you can wait for the opportunity to be discovered instead of creating it, but you need to be ready to wait for a possibly long time.

And you don't just create the opportunities, you prepare for them too. In the context of being discovered, this can mean having a brief pitch ready about your work and what sets you apart and having an initial fee or price to propose. After all, you don't want to encounter a prospective client and not have the details you need to close a deal.

So yes, luck can happen by accident, but if you look closely, the "luckiest" individuals—and the most powerful ones—are the people who create opportunities and prepare for them rather than wait for them and get caught by surprise.

> " Be prepared, work hard, and hope for a little luck. Recognize that the harder you work and the better prepared you are, the more luck you might have."
> — *ED BRADLEY*

EXERCISE

> "I'm a great believer in luck, and I find the harder I work, the more I have of it."
> — THOMAS JEFFERSON

Pick an area in your life where you want to be "lucky." It can be the area of your career, the area of your finances or the area of your relationships.

Then on a sheet of paper, create two columns. In the column on the left, list down all the opportunities you can create for yourself in this area. For instance, if the area is the area of your finances, opportunities you can write down can include: getting promoted at work, getting the chance to set up a side business, and so on and so forth.

Then in the column on the right, list down the all the ways you can think of to prepare for the opportunities you listed down in the column on the left. To go back to our earlier example, next to getting the chance to set up a side business, for instance, you can write down: learning how to manage a business, finding potential investors, and so on and so forth.

The final part of the exercise is for you to follow through on the ways of preparing that you listed down in the column on the right. So if you wrote down "learning how to manage a business," following through means signing up for a business management course, reading a book or getting the guidance of an expert.

I promise you, if you undertake this exercise faithfully, your luck—and your power—will expand by leaps and bounds.

QUESTIONS

1. In what areas of your life do you want to get really lucky?

2. Selecting just one of these areas, what would being lucky in this area look like for you precisely? Said another way, what would you want to happen?

3. What conditions would increase the probability of what you want to happen in this area actually happening?

4. What concrete actions can you take to bring these, or at least some of these, conditions to life?

5. What concrete ways can you prepare yourself to grab any opportunity that arises should these conditions actually come to pass?

22. THE POWER OF PEACE

FREEDOM FROM GUILT AND REGRET

In the chapter on ALIGNMENT, I talked about how conflicts with other people or within ourselves can lead to a lot of wasted time, energy and effort. This is because conflicts cancel our energies out: either someone's effort opposes ours, or, our own self-doubts paralyze or delay us.

In this chapter on PEACE, I'm going to talk about a different kind of conflict that weighs us down: not the conflict that comes from two agendas or two values countering each other, but the conflict that comes from not being at peace with ourselves because of guilt or regret.

Now, I'm a Roman Catholic by birth and upbringing, so I grew up being familiar with the notion of confession. For a long time though, I didn't understand the nature and purpose of the sacrament of confession. Things started getting clearer from me when I started to study different kinds of philosophical and religious systems. In the course of my research, I came across the Church of Scientology's system for dealing with what it calls "overts" (harmful actions) and "withholds" (harmful actions that we conceal). The process is similar to what you would go through in Catholic confession—the main difference is in the framework used for assessing what it is that you actually "confess." (The Catholic Church, for instance, would ask you to assess where you failed in terms of the Seven Sins or the Ten Commandments, whereas the Church of Scientology would ask you to assess yourself in terms of offenses against your family, offenses against your group, offenses against mankind, and so on and so forth.)

ARTWORK BY RENE TRINIDAD ALDONZA

The point is, when I went through the process, I started feeling incredibly lighter. And the impact wasn't confined to my psychological or spiritual well-being. The peace of mind I got as a result of the process literally allowed me to triple my sales results!

This might seem really strange to you at first, especially if you're used to separating the different areas of your life the way most people do. But what many people don't realize is that our feelings of guilt and regret about different things accumulate over the years and leave us carrying an increasingly heavier burden. We might not even be aware that we have such feelings, or when we are aware of them, we might not even take them seriously. But I assert that these feelings of guilt and regret are there and that they do have an impact. It's as if you're spending your life trying to win a hundred meter sprint not knowing that you're carrying a forty kilo weight on your back! Good luck with winning that race—it's simply not going to happen.

So whether you're a Catholic or a Scientologist or a believer of some other faith or even a non-believer, I suggest that you find a process that will allow you to get present to all the things you've held on to—all the things that we call "baggage" for very good reason—and begin letting them go. The healing and lightness you'll find as a result will be enormously rewarding in their own right. The fact that they'll also empower you in the other areas of your life—like in the area of your creative life, for instance—just happens to be a really big bonus.

> "Peace is not merely a distant goal that we seek, but a means by which we arrive at that goal."
> — *MARTIN LUTHER KING, JR.*

THE POWER OF PEACE

■ EXERCISE

> "There is no way to peace, peace is the way."
> — *A.J. MUSTE*

Take some time to sit down and start listing all the things in your life that you feel guilty about or that you regret doing or that you regret not doing. List down anything and everything for which you blame yourself, resent yourself or hold against yourself. List down all the perceived errors, failures, flaws, missed opportunities, mistakes and shortcomings. List everything down: when these incidents happened, where they happened, what their impact was on you and on other people, and what you could have done differently to handle the situation.

The point of this exercise is to allow you to literally purge yourself of all this baggage and negative energy by "confessing" or acknowledging to yourself what didn't work in your life. But by also having you look at what you could have done differently, the exercise is designed to leave you with power the next time you come across a similar situation. This way, you're not trapped by what happened in the past. Rather, the past becomes a guide to a more powerful future. You can then start the process of letting go.

Because if you think about it, what's happened has happened—there's no changing the past—and your guilt and regret will only poison your present and your future. Start to notice instead how all the "errors," "failures," "flaws," "mistakes" and "shortcomings" actually taught you things, built your character, made you a stronger person and brought you to where you are today. Start to acknowledge yourself for having done the best that you could have done in those past situations given the state of your knowledge and ability at those times. The point is: do what needs to be done so that you can be at peace with yourself, your past and the totality of your life.

Now, this is an enormously difficult exercise to do, and it's likely it will take several sessions. Take as long as you need and be patient with yourself. There are some things you won't want to remember and there are some things that will take a long time for you to remember. But you'll notice that as you keep going at it, you'll feel lighter and lighter, as if a burden that you never even knew existed was slowly being lifted. And when that weight is gone, all your attention and energy can now go into powerfully creating your present and your future.

QUESTIONS

1. Is there an area of life where you find yourself particularly burdened by guilt or regret?

2. Looking at this area, what about it can you recontextualize or interpret differently?

3. Continuing to look at this area, what lessons do you think it can offer you?

4. Still looking at this area, what can you forgive or simply let go?

5. What opens up for you as you complete answering the above questions?

23. THE POWER OF PRESENCE

PAYING ATTENTION

ARTWORK BY RENE TRINIDAD ALDONZA

When people talk about presence in the sense of having "presence of mind," they usually refer to someone's ability to masterfully handle an emergency.

What I find strange about this is that there's somehow an assumption that we only need our minds to be fully present whenever there's a crisis. Or, in the case of creative professionals, the assumption is that we only need our minds to be fully present whenever we're in the process of creating something (e.g., when we're writing, sketching, illustrating, designing, etc.). In most other situations, it seems as if it's okay if we're not really paying attention to what's going on.

I'm going to assert, however, that part of being powerful is being able to be fully present—to have full presence of mind—on an ongoing basis. Buddhism recognizes this, which is why it says that "mindfulness," or the state of being attentively aware of reality in the current moment, is the seventh element of the eightfold path to enlightenment.

The reason why being present is so critical to power is very simple: unless you really know what's going on, how can you effectively deal with any situation? And if you're not fully paying attention to things, how can you really know what's going on?

In other words, power depends on an accurate assessment of the situation, and an accurate assessment of the situation depends on close observation. So if you want to have power in any situation, start by being present. (I talk about something similar in the chapter on REALITY.)

The problem, however, is that we're not used to being present. In fact, it's not just that we're unused to being present—it's more like we're almost never present at all! The reason for this is that our attention is always being diverted by the constant chatter in our heads—at least when we don't have to focus in an emergency, or in a creative endeavor, or in some other serious task. This chatter is made up of all the thoughts and feelings and

THE POWER OF PRESENCE

> "The most precious gift we can offer others is our presence. When mindfulness embraces those we love, they will bloom like flowers."
> — THICH NHAT HANH

assessments and reactions and judgments and opinions that are always going on in our skulls. We're often so busy paying attention to all these internal rackets that we hardly have any attention left for what's going on outside. We function instead by going on auto-pilot—by letting mindless routines take over. You'll know what I mean if you think about how you are when you're driving. When you're driving, haven't you noticed that your mind usually wanders off to the meeting that you've got on your schedule, or to the food that you're having for lunch, or to the gift that you need to buy your wife, or to the appointment that you might miss . . . and so on and so forth? Very rarely are you fully paying attention to the act of driving, to what's on the road ahead of you or to the buildings that are flashing by outside your car. Given how absent your mind usually is when you drive, the only thing that will prevent you from getting into an accident is the speediness of your reflexes (so hopefully they're very fast!).

In my case, one area where I find myself not being present on occasion is when I'm coaching people! Sometimes, my thoughts will go somewhere else: I'll be anticipating the next question, or formulating my next answer, or worrying about how much money I'll make or how many more clients I'll get from the engagement. Sometimes, I'll go back to being present only to discover that it's my client who's not present!

That's why in my coaching engagements, one of the very first things I teach my clients is how to be present. Because if their mind or if my mind is somewhere else, no coaching will take place. They'll be saying something and I'll miss it, or I'll be saying something and they'll miss it. Or they might be saying something and intending something else, and I'll miss that. The point is, just like in any other situation in life, effectiveness and power in a coaching relationship depend on the parties' abilities to be present.

So if power depends on being present, and being present depends on being able to pay attention to things other than the constant chatter in our heads, then we start developing power by learning how not to be distracted by

> "As we let our light shine, we unconsciously give other people permission to do the same. As we are liberated from our own fear, our presence actually liberates others."
> – MARIANNE WILLIAMSON

the noise in our heads. And this is precisely what you'll get to do in the exercise below.

EXERCISE

It's important to know before you start this exercise that the noise in your head will never go away. You can't control your thoughts and you can't control your feelings. But the point of this exercise is not to stop the noise, but rather, to stop being distracted by it so that you can pay attention to other things for a change (like reality, for instance).

One method I've discovered that really works for me is to tell the voices in my head to "Go sit in the corner and have an ice cream and I'll come and get you when I'm done with what I'm doing." (This is very similar to a method I share in the chapter on COURAGE.)

Why this works is because it's very gentle and very lighthearted and there's no force or threat behind it. A variation that I also find very effective is to tell the voices in my head that "I really appreciate your inputs and I'll take them into account, but now I really need to focus." This works by acknowledging the reason why there are all those voices in your head to begin with—which is to fulfill your intentions in the best way they know how (have you noticed that the chatter is always about the things that matter to you?).

So just to be clear, it's not that the noise in your head is bad, it's just that it gets in the way of your being present.

Just one final note: it might seem a little strange to talk to yourself this way, but believe me, it works. The only thing I caution you to do is to not talk to yourself out loud!

OPTIONAL EXERCISE

This is an exercise you can do if you want to specifically develop an ability to be present to other people. It will involve other people though—or one other person at the very least.
First, find someone who's willing to be your partner in for this exercise. Then find a place where you won't be interrupted and face each other (preferably standing up) and look into each other's eyes.

Stay like this for at least three minutes.

Now, this is surprisingly difficult for a lot of people. In my coaching engagements, I've seen people daydream, fidget, giggle, laugh, look away, make faces and zone out—anything just to avoid having to be fully present to the other person!

So do this exercise fully and do it as often as necessary until you find yourself actually being present to the other person.

And then see what that provides for you in your life.

QUESTIONS

1. What are some of the things you do most often to escape from the present? These don't need to be dramatic—they can be as easy as daydreaming, eating, surfing the Internet, and so on and so forth.

2. When do you tend to zone out the most? Is it when you're feeling overwhelmed? Is it when you're feeling stressed? Or does it happen with no trigger at all?

3. What's the impact on you and your life when you escape from the present moment?

4. What would open up for you in your life if you could learn to be more mindful?

5. What small, practical and achievable practices could you take on daily to become more present to life? It can be as easy as taking up meditation, or focusing fully on your food when you eat, or focusing fully on the person you're speaking with when you're having a conversation. List down at least three practices.

24. THE POWER OF PURPOSE
A REASON FOR EXISTENCE

ARTWORK BY RENE TRINIDAD ALDONZA

On the broadest terms, purpose can be defined as the reason for which something exists. In my work as an executive coach, one of the things that really fascinate me is how organizations are so much more effective than individuals when it comes to articulating their purpose.

What do I mean?

Well, look at any organization. It can be the company you work for, or the charity you support, or the church you attend. I'm very sure that all of these will have a mission statement somewhere that includes a very clear and concise description of what the organization does or what its reason for existence is.

But if you ask the people you know what their purpose is, chances are that they won't be able to tell you. Or, if they can tell you, it won't be a very clear, concise and consistent answer.

I think the reason why organizations are better than individuals when it comes to articulating their purpose is because organizations are deliberate creations. That is, all organizations are born with a specific objective in mind. Companies are born because a person or a group of people have an objective to make a certain amount of money or to sell a particular kind of product or service. Non-profit organizations are born because a person has an objective to address a certain kind of social need. Social networks are born because people have an objective to remain connected with other people who have similar needs or interests.

In other words, organizations only come into being because people use them to fulfill certain intentions. These intentions can automatically serve as the purpose of the organization.

With people, on the other hand, it's different. None of us asked to be born. None of us came into being with a clear and definite idea of the purpose for which we were born. So unlike organizations that have intentions that are clear from the outset, human beings don't come with "automatic" intentions that can serve as guidelines for how we should live.

And this is okay when we're just starting out. When we're young, we don't have to worry about having a purpose yet. There's all that growing up and studying that needs to be done.

But once we reach a certain age and we're on our own, then having a purpose becomes absolutely critical.

Why?

Because without a purpose, we can easily spend the rest of our lives just running on auto-pilot, doing what our family wants or what society wants without really fulfilling a deeper or more meaningful intention. It's not that there's anything wrong with this, it's just that in my experience, people who live on auto-pilot don't live very happy lives. There's always a sense that "there's something missing" and that "there has to be more to life than this." It seems that people living without a purpose seem to be just floating along on the river of life. But when you think about it, even a dead fish can float along the river.

And, while having a purpose is absolutely critical to living a happy and fulfilling life, it's not always easy to discover or create a purpose. Some people are fortunate in that they find, very early in life, what it is that they were "born to do." Other people can spend years—even decades—on the search.

In my case, finding my purpose was a process that happened over several years. I knew that I'd finally found it when I created a statement of purpose that inspired me every time I read it or recalled it. Just thinking about the statement was enough to excite me and energize me. The statement I created was: "To be a trusted advisor to world leaders."

I created that statement ten years ago and since then my life has been nothing short of amazing. Creating that purpose gave me something to wake up for, to take action for and to look forward to. It gave me a sense of focus and direction. It gave me a WHY!

Before I created my purpose, I didn't know what to focus my life on: I was scattering my time and energy studying and learning different things without being clear on what exactly I was preparing myself for. When I discovered my purpose, it really funneled my time, energy and attention.

> "Start with the end in mind."
> — STEPHEN COVEY

Suddenly, I knew what kind of books to read, what kinds of people to meet and what kinds of skills to develop.

The other thing that discovering my purpose did for me besides simplifying and focusing my life was providing me with inspiration. I created my purpose ten years ago, and even if I've fulfilled it on several different levels already, it still inspires me and I still keep seeing new ways of expressing it in the world.

So whether it comes to you easily or not, finding your purpose is something that's a matter of urgency, because unless you're clear about your purpose in life, you'll be scattering your time, energy and attention on different things and in different directions. It's like being in a foreign city for the first time and not knowing what you want to accomplish as a tourist. Chances are, you'll spend hours just wandering around aimlessly, doing a little window shopping here and some sightseeing there, following the trail of some tourist groups here and following the trail of some locals there. In the end, you'll be tired and exhausted and you won't even have seen the best of what the city has to offer. On the other hand, if you were clear that your purpose was "to see the best museums and to eat the finest food in Paris," then a day-long itinerary would involve visiting the top three museums and the top three restaurants in Paris. There's no wasting time or money wandering around alleys or visiting churches or boating down rivers. It's museums and restaurants and that's it. Not that there's anything wrong with churches. I love churches and temples and any other house of God. But let's get back to what we're discussing here, which is purpose.

The same principle of having purpose applies to our lives—more so, in fact. We only have a limited amount of time on this earth, and if we want it to count for something, then we have to get clear about what we want to accomplish during the time that we have.
Some of you might be thinking: "But I really don't know what I want!"

If that's what's there for you, don't worry: you're not alone. The good news is that even if you can't think of a purpose for yourself, there are many things in your life that can point towards a possible purpose.

The first place to look at is all the things that you like doing or enjoy doing. The things that inspire and fulfill you are the biggest clues to what your purpose could be. You might be good at doing something, but if it doesn't inspire or fulfill you, chances are it's not your purpose.

Remember, your purpose is the reason for which you exist. So a good question to ask yourself when you're creating your purpose is: "What reason would be worth living for, or, what reason would be worthy of my existence? Or, what would be worth spending the rest of my life for? Or, how would I want to be remembered on my eightieth birthday? What kind of accomplishment do I want to be remembered for and what kind of legacy do I want to leave?"

The answers to these questions will lead you to your true purpose. And often the answers may not be an accomplishment at all. Sometimes it could be a way of being.

But what's the relationship between purpose and power?

What does purpose have to do with power?

First of all, just having a purpose is enormously empowering. Knowing what your life is about provides a tremendous amount of inspiration and motivation. When you're clear about your purpose, you can metaphorically (and even literally) move mountains.

Second, having a purpose allows you to focus all your time, energy and attention. Like I mentioned earlier, it serves as a guide for the choices you make and the actions you take, commitments you accept and even people you surround yourself with. In other words, having a purpose makes life simple—and that simplicity provides a lot of clarity, and with that clarity comes power.

A final word about purpose: once you have one, it's important to keep reminding yourself of it. In the same way that organizations put up copies of their purpose or mission on their office walls, it's advisable that you put a copy of your purpose somewhere where you can easily see it as well. That way, you can remind yourself time and again of what it is that your life is about.

EXERCISE

If you don't have a purpose yet, this is the time for you to create one. If you're not sure about what your purpose could be, start by listing down all the things that inspire you or fulfill you or that you enjoy doing. List everything down in a notebook. The list can be as long as you like. Don't censor yourself. Don't worry at this point about how the different things you enjoy seem to be contradicting another. Right now, what's important is that you get in touch with ALL the things that inspire or fulfill you.

Give yourself a week to work on this list because you might think of new things as the days go on.

After a week, review your entire list and start looking for themes. Do many of the items on your list have some logical connection to each other? Do many things seem to repeat themselves? If you're a creative professional, themes that are very likely to pop up are artistry and self-expression: you enjoy creating things that are new and/or different and expressing your personality, your ideas or your values through your creations. Rearrange your list so that the items are clustered around one or a few of these themes.

Once you've rearranged your list, examine it again. Is it possible that the themes you've come up with (if you have more than one) have an even deeper logical connection between them? Try to see if it's possible to unite all these themes into one over-arching purpose.

If you can't find a single over-arching purpose, then try to see which of the themes is most important to you. This theme may very well be your purpose. It doesn't mean that you now have to get rid of all the other themes—it just means that you should be prioritizing your time according to how important the themes are to you.

Once you have this "draft" purpose, test it. Put it up for a month and during that month, see if living your life by this purpose provides you with power, passion, simplicity and inspiration.

If it doesn't, it doesn't mean that you've failed—it just means that there's something that needs to be tweaked, or fine-tuned or further looked into. If it does, then congratulations! You are now living a life of purpose—a powerful life.

A note to those in organizations:

From my experience and my work with the world's largest organizations, I have found it to be one hundred times more powerful and inspiring to have a purpose rather than a mission.

A mission, in its purest sense, is just a statement of what the organization does. A purpose is a statement of why it does it. Disney's mission could have been to provide entertainment for the masses, but Disney didn't choose to have a mission. Instead, Disney chose a powerful purpose. The purpose Disney chose is "to make people happy." Now, it doesn't matter if I am a manager at Disney, or a cashier, or the person scrubbing the toilet. I can still be inspired to get out of bed in the morning because the purpose of my work is to make people happy, regardless of what I actually do. And for the sake of fulfilling that purpose, I can even gratefully scrub a toilet, or be a cashier, or sweep the street. Because it's not about what I'm specifically doing, but what I'm creating—which is happiness!

QUESTIONS

1. Do you have a clearly articulated purpose for your life? One that you've actually written down and can easily recall from the top of your head?

2. If you do have one, are you living a life that's consistent with your purpose? If not, what's getting in the way?

3. If you don't have one, what's been the impact on your life of not having a purpose? What's getting in the way of you creating one?

4. What actions can you take to either create a purpose or live your life more consistently with your purpose? List down at least five actions.

5. What do you think you'd gain if you lived a life of purpose or lived your life more consistently with your purpose?

"You and I want our lives to matter. We want our lives to make a real difference – to be of genuine consequence in the world. We know that there is no satisfaction in merely going through the motions, even if those motions make us successful or even if we have arranged to make those motions pleasant. We want to know we have had some impact on the world. In fact, you and I want to contribute to the quality of life. We want to make the world work."

— WERNER ERHARD

25. THE POWER OF REALITY

IN TOUCH WITH WHAT'S REALLY GOING ON

Few people live in reality. What I mean to say by that is that few people, very few people in fact, are actually in touch with what's really the case with things—with what's really going on. This applies to human beings in general and not just to creative people who, because of the nature of their work, do have to spend a lot of time inside their heads.

A lot of this has to do with something I talked about in the chapter on INTERPRETATION, which is that we automatically look at things in a certain way instead of as how they really are. For instance, people living in Manila will look out of their window and see the rain, and instead of seeing the rain as "water literally falling down from the sky," what they'll see instead is "lots and LOTS of horrendous traffic jams."

ARTWORK BY RENE TRINIDAD ALDONZA

Now in the chapter on INTERPRETATION, I talked about the power that comes from being able to choose our interpretation of reality. In this chapter, I'm going to focus on the power that comes from just confronting reality itself—the power, in other words, that comes from being able to see rain as rain and not as traffic or inconvenience or floods or colds.

Why there's power in seeing reality as it is is because we can then focus all our attention and energy on addressing it directly rather than getting distracted or disempowered by all our interpretations.

THE POWER OF REALITY

The Japanese, for instance, live in one of the most seismic regions of the world. Possible interpretations of this fact are "it's dangerous to live in Japan" or "you can't build high-rise buildings in Japan." The Japanese, however, have simply confronted the reality of their geography as it is—which is that it's earthquake-prone—and have accordingly developed the most advanced earthquake-resistance technologies in the world (while continuing to build many spectacular high-rise buildings).

At the same time, the Japanese have also suffered from not confronting reality as it is. The meltdown of the Fukushima Daiichi Nuclear Power Plant following the damage caused by the March 2011 Tōhoku earthquake and tsunami could have been avoided if the Tokyo Electric Power Company had heeded the warnings given by the United States Nuclear Regulatory Commission as early as 1990. The Fukushima disaster is currently the largest nuclear accident in history since the 1986 Chernobyl disaster and experts have estimated that it could take hundreds and potentially thousands of workers decades to clean up the effects of the meltdown. As you see from the examples I just gave, there's tremendous power in being able to see reality just as it is and then acting accordingly.

To go back to my earlier example, the Philippines is a tropical country and constant rain is therefore a reality in the country. And because the rain does seem to cause more traffic jams, traffic jams are therefore also a reality in the country.

At first, this was something I complained about along with

> "Common sense is the knack of seeing things as they are, and doing things as they ought to be done."
> — *C.E. STOWE*

everyone else. But when I realized that the traffic jams, like the rain, are just how things are in the Philippines (at least right now), I decided to address that reality directly rather than waste my time and energy in grumbling about it.

So what I did was I started listening to audio books in my car. I figured that if I was going to be spending a lot of time on the road, I could use that time very productively by using it as an opportunity to learn something new. Since then, my "reading" has stepped up from just one book a month (which was the average before I started listening to audio books) to up to two books a week!

Now, it's not an exaggeration for me to say that I actually enjoy my time on the road, because it's my time to learn something new for myself. But this is something I would never have come up with if I hadn't confronted and accepted reality just the way it is.

EXERCISE

> "The truth is not found in a different set of circumstances. The truth is always and only found in the circumstances you've got."
> — WERNER ERHARD

One area in life where I've consistently noticed people not dealing with reality is the area of their personal appearance. For example, cosmetic surgeons have reported that many patients still feel the same way about how they look even after they've had drastic adjustments made. So given that this is a particularly challenging area, I'm going to pick it as the area to focus on for this exercise.

The exercise consists of this: everyday, ideally several times in a day, get present to you in the mirror. Plant yourself in front of a mirror in an undisturbed place and get present to every detail of your face. Do this without squirming, without sighing, without flinching and without giving in to all the thoughts that automatically run through your head whenever you look in a mirror—thoughts like my nose is too big, my lips are too thin, my skin is too dull…and so on and so forth.

It's very likely that before this exercise, you've never taken a frank, straight look at your own face. Keep doing this until you get to the point where you can see your face and just see your face. And then see what that does for you.

QUESTIONS

1. What are some of your favorite ways of not dealing with reality? For instance, do you have a tendency to zone out by surfing the Internet when something unpleasant comes up? Do you distract yourself with alcohol, cigarettes or food? Do you hide in bed and go to sleep? Make your list as exhaustive as possible.

2. What's the impact on you whenever you escape from reality? What have the consequences been?

3. What stops you from confronting reality directly?

4. Picking one area of your life where you tend to escape reality, what small and practical actions can you take in this area to begin getting present to the facts?

5. What would it provide for you in this area if you learned to deal directly with reality?

26. THE POWER OF RESPONSIBILITY
BEING ACCOUNTABLE FOR SOMETHING

One of the standard dictionary definitions of responsibility is that it's the state of being accountable or "blame-able" for something.

Now most people understand what responsibility is, but I would also assert that most people don't understand how large the scope of their responsibility is. What I mean to say by that is that people generally limit their responsibility to things that they consciously choose. For example: "I chose to be a freelance writer, so I am responsible for the financial risks that come with being a freelance writer," or, "I chose to be wedding photographer, so I am responsible for the unpredictable demands on my time that come with being a wedding photographer."

Most people, however, never consider themselves responsible for things they didn't consciously choose.

For example, I spent a good part of my life dealing with a father who often told me that I wouldn't make it, that I'd never succeed and that I'd never amount to anything. I resented my dad because of this and spent many years blaming him for what I felt was my mediocre life. I never chose my dad—he was the dad I got—and I never chose the way he treated me. Therefore, I couldn't be held responsible for him and for the effects he had on me and my life.

Then one day, I heard my friend Anthony Robbins share the following story:

Once while the Buddha was traveling with his followers, a man who didn't like him started following him as well. The man would challenge the Buddha at every opportunity he got: attacking him, criticizing him and insulting him. This went on for days

ARTWORK BY RENE TRINIDAD ALDONZA

and weeks and months, until finally, the man approached the Buddha and said:

"I've been following you for months and I've attacked and criticized and insulted you at every chance I've found. But not once did you get affected by anything I said. Why not?"

The Buddha replied:
"May I ask you a question?"

THE POWER OF RESPONSIBILITY

> "Take your life in your own hands, and what happens? A terrible thing: no one to blame."
> — ERICA JONG

The man nodded.

So the Buddha went on: "If someone offers you a gift and you do not accept it, to whom then does the gift belong?"

The man responded: "It belongs to the person giving the gift."

The Buddha replied: "Precisely, so when someone gives you an insult, a challenge or a criticism and you do not accept it, to whom then does it belong?"

The man was silent, walked away and was never heard from again.

When I heard this story from Tony, I realized that even if I hadn't chosen my dad and even if I hadn't chosen how he looked at me, what I had chosen—without realizing it—was to accept his view of me. Just like me, the Buddha had never chosen the company of that man, and he hadn't chosen that man's dislike for him—but he did choose whether to accept that man's attacks or not.

It was in that moment that I got how you can actually be responsible for everything in your life, even if there are many things in your life that you never consciously chose. By assuming responsibility for the entirety of your life, you take back and return to yourself the power that circumstances would otherwise have in determining your happiness and fulfillment. Whenever you take responsibility for something, blame disappears—and power emerges. As it turns out, both blaming and taking responsibility are habits. Blaming is the habit of victims, while taking responsibility is a habit of winners.

> "Let everyone sweep in front of his own door, and the whole world will be clean."
> — JOHANN WOLFGANG VON GOETHE

EXERCISE

Look into your life and see what "gifts" life has given you that you've accepted (consciously or otherwise). Make a list and see which of these "gifts" you really want in your life and which ones you want to send back.

How do you send "gifts" back? Simple: you choose not to accept them. There's nothing else you have to do. Notice that the Buddha didn't blame the man for being who he was, and he certainly didn't blame himself for having somehow allowed the man into in his life. He simply took responsibility by not accepting an unwanted gift.

OPTIONAL EXERCISE

Whenever you find yourself blaming someone or something or feeling disempowered, helpless and weak, sit down and start brainstorming on the ways that you can be the "cause" of the situation.
Now, don't do this just so that you can shift the blame onto yourself! This is not about shifting blame but about making it disappear altogether.

The point of looking for ways that you can be the "cause" of the situation is so that you can then look for ways to actually DO something about the situation. Simply adopting the point of view of a powerless victim will do nothing except leave you being exactly that: POWERLESS. When you accept responsibility, you take on being cause in the matter. When you are cause in having created the situation than you can also un-create that situation. You can now truly be the master of life as you experience it. You can now truly transform the experience of your life and in that you have now become the master of your destiny.

QUESTIONS

1. What areas or aspects of your life have you "not chosen" and therefore cannot be held responsible for?

2. In each of these areas, whom have you blamed or held responsible for the state of affairs in each area?

3. What's your experience of life like in these areas?

4. Selecting just one of these areas, what would you need to do to retake responsibility for this area of your life?

5. What begins to open up for you as you take on being fully responsible for this area of your life?

27. THE POWER OF TRUST

AFFINITY, COMMUICATION AND SHARED REALITY

In my experience as a trainer and coach to senior executive teams, the one thing that's usually missing the most is trust amongst colleagues. I've witnessed many instances where relationships have deteriorated so much that executives on the same team have stopped talking to each other for as much as two or even three years! In these cases, restoring trust amongst team members has the single greatest effect on boosting the level of their performance.

Trust is a function of integrity and authenticity (both of which we cover in a different chapters) but it can also be enhanced in other ways.

One of the most effective tools that I've discovered is what L. Ron Hubbard calls the ARC Triangle. Hubbard is known as the founder of the Church of Scientology and while his life may have attracted a lot of controversy, some of the tools that he developed—including the ARC Triangle—have proven to be remarkably robust.

ARTWORK BY RENE TRINIDAD ALDONZA

The letters A, R and C in the ARC Triangle refer to affinity, reality and communication. Very roughly, affinity refers to the affection between people; reality to the world that they share; and communication to the exchanges between them. According to Hubbard, increasing any one of the three also increases the other two.

For example, if I share my world with someone else more often, the increase in our shared reality will increase the regard we have for each other and the quality of the communication between us. By continuously working on any one of the three, the other two increase accordingly and the increases can quickly build up into a virtuous upward spiral. However, the opposite also holds true. By allowing any one of the three to deteriorate, the other two deteriorate as well. And if the deterioration isn't addressed, a vicious downward spiral can be the result.

What does this have to do with trust? Very simply, when we have high levels of affinity, communication and shared

> "You may be deceived if you trust too much, but you will live in torment if you do not trust enough."
> — *FRANK CRANE*

reality between people, we have a solid foundation for building trust among them. Hence, the ARC Triangle provides an immediate and straightforward access to cultivating one of the most essential elements of power, which is simply the element of trust.

For creative professionals who have to work as part of a team, establishing this kind of trust between team members is especially critical because producing a creative work is radically different from, say, assembling a car. A creative endeavor is always more than the sum of its parts, and the process itself is organic—meaning to say, it arises spontaneously out of the interactions of the people involved. So the more the members of a creative team trust each other, the more synchronized their efforts become, and the better the overall result.

For me personally, one of the areas in my life where I've found applying the ARC Triangle to be very effective is the area of prospecting for clients. In the past, when I would do "cold calls" or "cold emails" to prospective clients, I'd usually just stick to sharing my accomplishments when it came to the part about sharing my credentials. Then when I started applying the ARC Triangle, specifically the part about increasing my shared reality with others, I started saying a little bit more about myself beyond just my achievements. I'd talk a little bit about being a husband or a father or some of my other experiences in life, like the movie I saw the night before, or the weather as I experienced it going to work. Just doing this had a tremendous impact on the rate of responses from prospective clients!

In general, I think that many of our business interactions have become very mechanical. When we're working, we relate to other people—and get related to by other people—as an issue to address, an ordeal to survive, a transaction to complete or a signature to collect. Worse, we relate to each other as machines. When we share something about ourselves that isn't related to the work, it actually humanizes the experience. Suddenly, we're not cogs in the machine interacting with other cogs in the machine. People appreciate that injection of warmth and humanity into the interaction and that's why they're likelier to respond.

For me, I not only enjoy the fact that I get more responses. I also enjoy it when other people respond to what I'm sharing by sharing something of themselves as well! That's when things get really fun, interesting and rewarding.

EXERCISE

Next time you find yourself speaking to a stranger, whether in a personal or professional context, share a little bit about what's going on in your life with him or with her. It doesn't have to be particularly serious or significant—it can be as mundane as the weather, a film you just watched or an incident with your children.
Whatever it is, try sharing more about yourself than usual—and see how the increase in shared reality leads to more affinity, communication and trust with the person to whom you're speaking.

OPTIONAL EXERCISE

Another exercise I recommend is something that I use in my work in coaching executive teams. This exercise typically makes the biggest difference in restoring trust amongst executive team members.

As I mentioned earlier in the chapter, one way to increase trust is to increase the shared reality between people—that is, to have people share their perspective of life or of a situation with the people around them. However, there's a way of sharing one's reality that can backfire by actually increasing the hostility between people—and that's by sharing one's reality from the perspective of blaming.

What this looks like is this: "It's hard for me to get my job done when you never give me clear instructions ahead of time and when you keep changing direction…" and so on and so forth. So to actually generate trust when sharing one's reality, it's best to share reality in what I refer to as a constructive, future-based manner. That is, instead of having people share what they don't want or don't like, especially in another person (e.g., "you never take the initiative"), I ask them to share what they do like or what they do want in another person and to say it in the future tense if necessary (e.g., "you could really increase your effectiveness if you took the lead in the projects you're handling").

The point is that people never like to hear what's wrong with them, even if that feedback is shared with the best of intentions. But people will always be interested in hearing how they can be more effective or more successful, and they'll greatly appreciate your contributions in this area. You'll be amazed to see what a simple exercise in sharing reality from a constructive, future-based perspective can do for the level of affinity and trust in a team.

QUESTIONS

1. What relationships in your life are marked by an absence of trust?

2. Selecting one of these relationships, ask yourself if any or all of the following elements are missing: affinity, reality and communication.

3. Working with the element that's missing or missing the most, what actions can you take on to address the gap? List at least five actions.

4. What would it provide for you to restore trust in this relationship?

5. What would it provide for the other person if trust was restored in this relationship?

28. THE POWER OF VISION
WHERE YOU WANT TO GO

When you don't know where you want to end up, it doesn't matter much where you're going or in what direction you're headed. Not having a vision about where we want to go in work or in life almost always ensures you won't get there.

On the other hand, having a clear vision will help you focus on the desired outcome and help you attract that outcome. The first time you formulate your vision, you may not be ready to articulate one that's really "out there" and that truly inspires you. You may not yet have experienced the power of having a vision and you therefore feel skeptical or doubtful about the process. This would be the time to let go of those doubts and proceed with faith.

A vision can be expressed as a statement, as a picture, as a collage or as a drawing. Given that you're a creative professional, find a means of articulating or expressing your vision that works best for you!

Most organizations, however, will prefer a written vision statement over a visual representation, but even in these cases, the written statement can be supplemented with a visual created by a team. The process of creating the visual—as well as the visual itself—can help make the vision more real in the minds of team members, thereby making the vision more motivating and much easier to fulfill.

Now, the most powerful and inspiring vision statements are very specific. They usually state by when and where the vision will be accomplished. They are also almost always a good stretch beyond what we believe we can accomplish. Finally, they

ARTWORK BY RENE TRINIDAD ALDONZA

are short statements that people can easily remember (a vision statement that people can't remember is practically useless).

When working with teams, it's important to ensure that everyone is aligned with the vision. If the vision was just developed by the head of the team, the team members may not be aligned at all, or, their level of alignment may be much lower than it could have been had they been co-creators of the vision. When

■ EXERCISE

people only "buy in" on a verbal level, this is called lip service—meaning to say they've expressed alignment but are not actually or fully aligned. When this happens, the true power of having a vision is not realized. So even if it takes a lot of time and effort, it's worth the resources invested to have all the people involved in an organization, a group or a project co-create a vision.

> "The pain will push you until the vision pulls you."
> — *Rev. Dr. MICHAEL BERNARD BECKWITH*

Next time you find yourself speaking to a stranger, whether in a personal or professional context, share a little bit about what's going on in your life with him or with her. It doesn't have to be particularly serious or significant—it can be as mundane as the weather, a film you just watched or an incident with your children.

Whatever it is, try sharing more about yourself than usual—and see how the increase in shared reality leads to more affinity, communication and trust with the person to whom you're speaking.

QUESTIONS

1. Which of the groups or organizations you're involved with in life have a clear vision?

2. What's your experience like working with or being involved with these organizations?

3. Which of the groups or organizations you're involved with have no clear vision?

4. What's your experience like working with or being involved with these organizations?

5. Reflecting on your previous answers, what actions can you take for yourself in your own life? Are you ready to create a vision (if you don't have one) or are you ready to take your vision to a new level?

AFTERWORD

So there you have it: twenty-eight ways of being with which to generate power so that you can achieve, accomplish and create things beyond your wildest dreams. You might not be able to integrate all these ways of being into your life all at once. That's completely fine. Just take on as many as you're comfortable with, maybe even just one at a time, and practice that way of being for as long as it takes until it becomes a habit. You will know when this has happened when it has become natural to you.

Then take on another one (or another set). Sometimes my wife and I will pick some just for a specific occasion. We may ask each other who we'll need to be to make a certain event or outcome successful and we may just choose three or four for the moment. After the event we always check and see if we succeeded in being what we had chosen to be before the event. And it's almost always a match. When you're done with all of them and we're never really done practicing—go right back to the start and practice them all over again. It's an ongoing process and an ongoing journey. The beautiful thing about it is: it's the kind of journey where it's the process and the experience of traveling that counts rather than the destination.

So have fun on your journey and enjoy the trip! I look forward to accompanying you time and again.

ABOUT THE AUTHOR

Bjorn C. Martinoff is an Executive Coach working with the world's most senior leaders. He is the President of F1C International, a company focusing on Executive and Organization Development and has created turnarounds and accelerated success for several of the world's largest and most famous companies. He is also the President and founder of F1CN, the Fortune 100 Coaches Network, and ODPNi the Organization Development Professionals Network International. Bjorn has worked with the following companies: Samsung, Sony, Mercedes-Benz, Mitsubishi, Nestle, Unilever, Intel, UBS, Cognizant, Boehringer-Ingelheim, Eli Lilly, NCO, Ovaltine, Twinings, Citigroup, Sanofi Pasteur, Mead Johnson, Zuellig Pharma, Pfizer, Bristol-Myers Squibb, Unilab, Asian Development Bank, Johnson & Johnson, L'Oreal, Avon, IBM, Intel, Maersk Line, Speedo, San Miguel, Nokia, Dell, Logica, One World Connections, Navitaire, Cypress, Sunpower, SGS, Caterpillar, Baker & McKenzie, Pharma Industries, and many others. Bjorn currently resides in Asia with his wife Victoria and their four children Minday, Maxwell, Malcolm, and Sarah.

You can find out more Bjorn Martinoff or contact him at the following websites:

www.fortune100coach.com

and

www.f1c-international.com

SOME BOOK RECOMMENDATIONS

Recommended reads and other sources of inspiration:

The E-Myth by Michael Gerber

The Celestine Prophecy by James Redfield

Conversations with God – Book 1 to 3, by Neale Donald Walsch

Any books, seminars, and audiobooks by Anthony Robbins

Feel the Fear and do it anyways by Susan Jeffers

The Landmark Forum by Landmark Education Corporation

And many more.

www.ingramcontent.com/pod-product-compliance
Lightning Source LLC
Chambersburg PA
CBHW041831300426
44111CB00002B/52